Library of
Davidson College

Bruno Mario Damiani

Montemayor's *Diana*, Music, and the Visual Arts

Madison, 1983

ADVISORY BOARD OF THE HISPANIC
SEMINARY OF MEDIEVAL STUDIES, LTD.

Samuel Armistead
Theodore S. Beardsley
Diego Catalán
Jerry Craddock
Alan D. Deyermond
Brian Dutton
Charles Faulhaber
Ian Macpherson
Margherita Morreale
Hans-J. Niederehe
Harvey Sharrer
John K. Walsh
Raymond S. Willis

Copyright © 1983 by
The Hispanic Seminary of
Medieval Studies, Ltd.

ISBN 0-942260-28-7

To my mother

Photographic reproduction: Gold enamelled pendant, in a boat shape, probably of Venetian work, is similar to the naviform earrings worn by Felismena in Book IV of *La Diana*. Courtesy of the Victoria and Albert Museum, London. Crown copyright.

Table of Contents

Introduction 1

Chapter I Music in *La Diana* 7

Chapter II *La Diana* and the Visual Arts 33

Conclusion 89

Notes 91

Introduction

Along with a renewed interest in classical archeology, philosophy, and literature, the Renaissance brought on an intensification of interest in music and musical instruments. Sixteenth-century theorists, novelists, poets, and dramatists cited the authority of Plato, Aristotle, and Pythagoras; repeated the anecdotes of Plutarch on the power of music to excite or placate human passions; evoked the legend of Mercury as inventor of the lyre; and recounted the myth of Orpheus, who tamed beasts and demons with the sweet sounds of his lyre and song.[1] In the prologue to his *Orphénica lyra*, Miguel de Fuenllana speaks of the great esteem in which music was held by the Greeks, noting that to them he who did not know how to play and sing was scorned, regardless of his eminence in the field of letters.[2]

While buttressing their fondness for music with the authority of the ancients, Renaissance humanists explored new ways of elevating and exalting the word with the sound of music. With the sixteenth century, Spain, in particular, enters into its Golden Age of music and musical instruments, which declines in the following century as painting takes up the scepter of the arts.[3] The Renaissance experiences the most glorious stages of Spanish music with such figures as Francisco Salinas, Antonio de Cabezón, and the great polyphonists of the Sevilian and Castilian schools, Cristóbal Morales, Francisco Guerrero, and Tomás Luis de Victoria.

One author who partook fully in the musical excitement of the time was Jorge de Montemayor, best known for his pastoral novel, *Los siete libros de la Diana* (Valencia, 1559). Living in a period called "the most brilliant epoch in the history of European music,"[4] Jorge de Montemayor left his native Portugal and went to Spain to become a chapel singer, first in the court of Charles V, and then in that of Philip II. In his *Exposición moral sobre el psalmo LXXXVI del real propheta David* (1548), dedicated to Princess Maria, first daughter of Charles V, Montemayor calls himself "cantor en la capilla de Su Majestad [Maria]" (ed. F. López Estrada, *Revista de Bibliografía Nacional*, 5 [1944], 509). Archival documents reveal that upon the death of Maria, Montemayor was named "contrabajo" in the chapel of her sister, Princess Juana, distinguished protectress of writers and artists.[5]

Because of the paucity of information about Montemayor's life and family background, it has been hypothesized that his mother or grandmother may have been a Spanish singer of Jewish origin.[6] One of the earliest literary demonstrations of Montemayor's penchant for music is found in the last of his three "autos" where simple, rustic characters end their contemplation of the meaning of Christ's birth with a humorous musical game, "passa, barbado," the words of which eulogize several Scriptural figures through references to their beards and wisdom, or lack of it.[7] Montemayor further underscores his musical inclination in a poem in which he admits his weakness in the humanities but stresses his fondness for music, a discipline in which, he says, "gasté mi tiempo todo."[8] In the poem, intended as a letter to the renowned Portuguese poet, Francisco Sâ de Miranda, Montemayor refers to music as a God-given talent, which has provided him not only with joy, but the means of his livelihood as well. In his reply to Montemayor's verse letter, Sâ de Miranda commends the future author of *Diana* for his musical ability, noting that by his singing he could move his audience to joy or tears.[9] It was this talent which won Montemayor access into the highest social circles of his times, including the Spanish and Portuguese courts.

In the service of Philip II, notable patron of Spanish music, Montemayor was able to cultivate his voice and expand his knowledge of instruments to the point that he came to be held in singular esteem by the royal family,[10] no small accomplishment for a foreigner in a choir made up exclusively of Spaniards, with the exception of the French composer Philippe de Monte who temporarily joined the choir between 1554-1555.[11] Like the great musicians and singers of the court of Philip II, Montemayor had travelled extensively to many parts of Europe including Naples, the residence of the Spanish viceroys. These journeys represented an unquestionably fecund source of information on musical techniques and styles. Let us be mindful of the fact that music, painting, and architecture had joined together in Italy to make that country a paradise of the plastic and lyrical arts.[12] While at court, Montemayor became knowledgeable about the best musical figures of the time, including Antonio de Cabezón, composer of the most important organ tablature of the sixteenth century, the *Obras de música para tecla, arpa y vihuela* (Madrid, 1578). Like the author of *Diana*, Cabezón accompanied Philip II on his brief nuptial interlude in England.[13]

It has been said that the sixteenth century was a pioneering era for composers, theorists and, by extension, for singers.[14] On this basis there is no doubt that Montemayor enjoyed the new spirit of experimentation and discovery. As Boscán and Garcilaso launched the adaptation of Italian meters into Castilian poetry, so Montemayor propels a variety of courtly instruments onto the Spanish pastoral state. As Titian, musician as well as painter, had "accorded equal dignity to the senses of hearing and of sight,"[15] Montemayor, musician and master of literary portraiture, imbues his novel with a distinct lyricism. For this reason, *Diana* shares much with the pastoral fable introduced in the Italian Renaissance by Poliziano and Sannazzaro's *Arcadia*. These "provided an opportunity to focus attention less on possibly debatable content than on lyric poetry, opulent settings, and music."[16]

Unlike other authors of pastoral novels, including Cervantes, who make reference to instruments mentioned in the works of their predecessors,[17] Montemayor speaks of instruments about which he learned professionally, and which he saw and heard in his everyday life. In a way that brings to mind Gil Vicente, who amply reflects his knowledge of music in his *Autos y Farsas*,

Montemayor conveys his musical expertise in *Diana*. Of the twenty-three instruments listed in the inventory of musical instruments used in the court of Charles V and Philip II,[18] twelve are mentioned in *Diana*. The novel is filled with references to music, songs, and musical instruments, and also mentions of dancing. These allusions appear universally, not only in the context of shepherds, shepherdesses, and nymphs, but of urban figures as well.

True to the Platonic view (*Symposium*, 212 B3) that *erós* supplies a fuel, of suprapersonal origin, to help make music, the enamoured shepherds of *Diana* energetically pursue singing and piping, in a way that gives credence to the view that in singing, "the herdsman is not doing anyone a favor; he is pleasing himself."[19] The musical domain of *Diana* includes the rustic tunes of the pipe or flute, as well as the nobler, "uplifting harmonies"[20] of stringed instruments and polyphonic song. The poetry of shepherds was written, after all "for and by sophisticates...the shepherd in pastoral literature is, strictly speaking, never a shepherd. He is a musician, a poet, a prince, and a priest."[21] Overwhelmed by the music played by his characters, Montemayor resorts to describing its sound as either "tan dulcemente que no hay sabello dezir" (p. 179), or in terms that evoke a supernatural quality: "divinamente," "cosa del cielo" (p. 231) or simply "celestial" (p. 72).

Despite the Platonic position that sight is the noblest and most accurate of all senses (*Timaeus*, 47 A-D, *Phaedrus*, 250 D), Montemayor combines the visual perception of his characters with a preponderance of acoustic experience. Clearly, the author of *Diana* would take issue with Leonardo da Vinci's view that "music is to be termed only a sister of painting, for it is subject to the sense of hearing, a sense second to the eye."[22] To Montemayor, musician, the auditory experience must surely have been as important as sight itself, much as it was for Marsilio Ficino, who "proposed a reasonable compromise"[23] on the highly debated issue, in the Renaissance, of the respective importance of the senses. Attributing equal honor to the senses of sight and hearing, Ficino states: "There are three kinds of beauty, that of the soul, that of the body and that of sounds; that of the soul is perceived by the mind, that of the body we perceive through the eyes, that of sound through the ears; love is always content with the mind, the eyes and the ears."[24]

In his portrayal of the pastoral world of *Diana*, Montemayor also employs terms common to the pictorial arts, pictorial themes are injected in the prose and poetry of the novel, and visual elements of color, light, shade and perspective abound as do references to fabrics, precious metal, stones and jewels. This pictorial tendency makes Montemayor a writer-painter whose *Diana* betrays a structure that resembles "the interweaving of various themes in a tapestry,"[25] and the characters all appear in "primer plano," in the words of Enrique Moreno Báez, "como unas figuras de los tapices."[26] The novel's rich and varied literary design is the art with which the author welds together form and content, symbolic significance and aesthetic effect, and creates several incidents which find corresponding images in the visual arts.

Chapter I

Music in *La Diana*

1

The first reference to music in *Diana* is made at the beginning of Book I when the disconslate Sireno takes up his rebec and sings to some "golden locks" of Diana's hair which he has been guarding in his breast "¡Cabellos, quánta mudança / he visto después que os vi!" (ed. F. López Estrada, Madrid, 1945, pp. 13-14). Originally a rustic instrument, the rebec was widely used by minstrels and travelling singers in the Middle Ages. By the late fifteenth and early sixteenth centuries it had acquired a more developed form, and a notable importance in courtly circles as well. It was esteemed by Ferdinand and Isabel, the Catholic monarchs, for example, and by Philip II, in whose musical inventory there was conspicuously present "un rabelico de madera laqueado, colorado y oro, y la tapa de madera, blanca dorada, sin cuerdas ni porteçuela-es hecho en la China."[1]

Much-cultivated in the Renaissance (although virtually absent from the Florentine *intermedii* of the sixteenth century),[2] the rebec appears in *Diana* with a frequency suggestive of its importance in the courtly musical life of sixteenth-century Spain. Sireno sings to the accompaniment of a rebec again in Book I, where, we read, "Luego, el olvidado Sireno començó a cantar al son de su rabel..." (p. 60), and again "Esto Sireno cantava / y con su rabel tañía" (p. 76). He is praised for his "dulces versos" (p. 10), attesting that in the pastoral, "song is not a present but a natural event, a spontaneous way of voicing the feelings and longings that press for recognition."[3] As the shepherd's singing is qualified, so are the musical instruments mentioned in *Diana*, e.g. "dulce çampoña o flauta" (p. 41); "loçano rabel" (p. 270). Similarly, instruments are cared for: "rabel que muy pulido en un çurrón siempre traya" (pp. 9-10), and "mi rabel preciado" (p. 86).

To alleviate their suffering, shepherds constantly sing, for, as Petrarch noted, "cantando il duol si desacerba."[4] Accordingly, Sireno's erstwhile rival, Sylvano, takes up his bagpipe, plays a while, and then sings "con gran tristeza," sentiments of his unrequited love for Diana in a poem that begins with the memorable verse "Amador soy, mas nunca fui amado" (pp. 16-18). In the courtly framework of *Diana* the bagpipes are introduced to create an especially characteristic rustic effect. The intimate relationship of the shepherds and shepherdesses to their music leads to a personified treatment of the musical instrument, true companion and ever-present source of comfort: "Venid vos acá, çampoña," calls Selvagia as she takes her bagpipe into her hand, "y passaré con vos el tiempo que si yo con sola vos lo uviera passado, fuera de mayor contento para mí..." (p. 64).

Shepherds know their verses by heart (p. 22). They have a prodigious memory, "bordering on total recall," as R.G. Keightley notes, "especially for music and verse."[5] This is exemplified in the opening pages of *Diana* where Sylvano reveals that he has eavesdropped on Sireno and Diana as the two lovers were delighting each other with lyrical sentiments by the banks of a stream. In that situation Sylvano hears a song of his rival Sireno, and commits to memory a written text later dropped by Diana. At Sireno's urging, he repeats those memorable verses (p. 22).

Sylvano again overhears and memorizes a song, this time one of Diana's, as she laments her separation from Sireno in a long poem in which past presence and joy are firmly juxtaposed to present absence and anguish (pp. 25-27). Significantly, Diana's song, as reported by Sylvano, "Ojos que ya no veys...", was set to music by Ginés de Morata, chapel master in the Ducal House of Braganza, and may be found, along with its musical rendition, in the opulent collection of Spanish secular polyphonic music of the *Cancionero Musical de la Casa de Medinaceli* (Madrid, Biblioteca de la Casa del Duque de Medinaceli, sign. 13230;

modern transcription and study by Miguel Querol Gavaldá, Barcelona, 1949, I, 63-66).

Later, Sireno and Sylvano again take out their instruments, one the rebec, the other the bagpipe, and alternately play and sing "con mucha gracia y suavidad" (p. 30). Then Sireno, Sylvano and Selvagia overhear the conversation of the three nymphs, followed by the song of the nymph Dórida, which, to the astonishment of Sireno, recounts his parting from Diana (pp. 72-73). The song, we soon learn, had been composed by one Celio, "que desde encima de un roble los estava acechando y la puso toda al pie de la letra en verso, de la misma manera que ella passó" (p. 73). So ardently fond of music and song are the characters of *Diana* that they poeticize and put into music not only their own feelings but also, as Celio demonstrates, the conversations of others.

Shortly after putting en end to their sad song, Sireno and Sylvano see, coming from the thicket near the river, "una pastora tañendo con una çampoña y cantando con tanta gracia y suavidad como tristeza" (p. 34). She is Selvagia who, in recounting her story of love, makes reference to another instrument of the pleasance: the flute (p. 41). Of the various types of flutes, the one to which Selvagia is most likely referring is what was known in Spain as "flauta recta" (i.e., recorder), also called "flauta dulce" or "flauta pastoril."[6] In the course of her story, Selvagia gives further evidence of the rustic urge to music, as she narrates: "Comencé yo con gran confiança a tocar mi çampoña, cantando la canción que oyreis" (p. 57). Music continues to the end of Book I where Alanio's first song to Ysmenia is accompanied by the sound of his rebec: "No más, Nympha cruel, ya estás vengada..." (pp. 53-54), and Sireno once again uses his rebec to accompany a song to his grieving eyes: "ojos tristes, no lloreys..." (pp. 60-61).

The second book opens with a long complaint of Selvagia's, after which she plays the bagpipe and sings some *sestinas* that begin with the verse: "Aguas que de lo alto desta sierra" (pp. 64-66). Sylvano reappears, singing octaves to the music of a rebec "Cansado está de oírme el claro río" (pp. 66-68). As Sireno and Selvagia discuss the suffering brought on by their respective cases of love, the "olvidado" Sireno is heard singing a sonnet to the tune of his rebec: "Andad, mis pensamientos, do algún día" (pp. 70-71). Also in Book II the nymph Dórida, singing with her harp of the original love of Diana and Sireno, recounts how Sireno gave Diana his shepherd's crook and his rebec, to which he used to sing her perfections (p. 86). Consonant with their characterization as noble women, the nymphs do not play rustic instruments, only the harp and similar courtly instruments, as we shall see below.

Several scenes of *Diana* are reminiscent of tableaux, those elaborate scenic interludes of the time that came complete with "ingenious stage machinery"[7] as well as music and dancing. One such scene is that of Celia being serenaded by Felix and a group of friends, a festival intended to celebrate Felix's union with his newly acquired beloved (pp. 105-110). This scene, like comedies with *intermedii*,[8] includes details about the elaborate set (complete with balcony), rich costumes, and courtly music, all those elements which will make up the early opera of the seventeenth century and have been characteristic of opera ever since.[9] At its simplest the serenade to Celia reminds us of the way a "madonna" ("honorable courtesan") was wooed by Renaissance nobles and wealthy persons. In the sixteenth century madrigals addressed to a "madonna" were often serenades, and as such were meant to be performed out of doors, primarily by voices, and—like most other madrigals—with one voice on each part. Felismena, witnessing the complimentary performance, remarks: "Y luego, començó una voz cantando a mi parecer lo mejor que nadie podría pensar" (p. 106).

While "composers of secular music during the Renaissance did not generally write with specific combinations of voices and instruments in mind,"[10] contemporary descriptions of performances, including those found in *Diana*, explicitly point out that much vocal music was accompanied by instruments appropriate to the situation and the individuals playing them. In the episode of Celia's serenade, there is mention of an opulent array of musical instruments, including the harp, viols, and cornets, in a way that brings to mind the many references to music and instruments in sixteenth-century booklets dealing with Italian court entertainment, which list in detail instruments accompanying singers of specific compositions.[11] Felix, a nobleman, is first heard singing with the accompaniment of courtly instruments, a harp and a "dulzaina" (p. 107). The latter was a small trumpet or "reed," characterized by its nasal and penetrating tone quality, which, as a member of the shawm family, was an ancestor of the oboe, formed in the early part of the seventeenth century. Felix then sings a sonnet "Gastando fué el amor mis tristes años" (p. 108) while playing the harp. Following his song, the serenade for Celia continues with a *canción* arrangement of four "vihuelas de arco" (probably "violas de gamba") and a "clavicordio" (term applied to the "harpsichord," in sixteenth century Spain).[12]

The festive song is riddled with echoes of "engaño" and "desengaño," a problematic at the heart of the novel itself. The performance is carried on "tan concertadamente," notes Felismena, "que no sé si en el mundo pudiera aver cosa más para oír ni qué maior contento diera a quien la tristeza no tuviera tan sojuzgada como a mí" (p. 109).

The propriety of the harp in scenes dealing with women's love and virtue has already been pointed out by Miguel Querol Gavaldá,[13] and with respect to Celia's staged serenades, it should be noted that at the first intermission of a Golden Age comedia, a "baile" was sung and danced, to the accompaniment of "vihuela," harp, and other instruments.[14] Music for the "vihuela," either alone or as accompaniment, was an art of classical inspiration, and in this a magnificent artistic expression of humanism.[15] The "vihuelistas" looked upon their instrument as the descendant of the classical lyre, or rather as the lyre itself, in its modern form;[16] they therefore conceived of music for voice with "vihuela" accompaniment as a resurrection of the classical song accompanied by the lyre.[17] Not suprisingly, Miguel de

Fuenllana praises the "vihuela" above all other instruments, not only for its sound, but, more importantly, for its exceptional ability to give relief and clarity to the letter,[18] to enhance the "effect" of the song, fulfilling with that an important humanistic aspiration.

The "vihuela," an early form of the guitar, had just become an important instrument during Montemayor's life. Partly responsible for the success of that instrument in Spain was the theoretician Luis de Narváez, author of *Los seys libros del Delphín de música / de cifras para tañer vihuela* (Valladolid, 1538). A member of the retinue that accompanied Philip II in his first journey to Italy, Germany, and Flanders, Narváez also served as chapel master of the Spanish court between 1549 and 1550.[19] Montemayor, who had formed part of that retinue and was a singer in that same court, was undoubtedly enlightened by Narváez, not only with respect to the "vihuela," but quite possibly about other musical instruments as well. In the sixteenth century three types of "vihuelas" coexisted: "vihuela de mano," "da arco," and that of the plectrum. The most widely used was the "vihuela de mano." The "vihuela da arco," played like a jig or a rebec, was the older and more popular form of the more recent "vihuela da mano," which was played with the fingers and was used in Italy, as in Spain, only since the beginning of the sixteenth century. The popularity enjoyed in the Renaissance by vocal soloist with "vihuela" accompaniment,[20] has been pointed out by Gustave Reese, and it is worth noting that Luis Milán, a composer with poetic pretensions, wrote an entire book entitled *El Maestro* (Valencia, 1536), dealing with the uses of the "vihuela da mano," which he identified as an instrument with six courses and ten frets, while the "vihuela" of Juan Bermudo (1549) had seven chords.

Significantly, the "vihuela" had been selected by one of the best musicians of the sixteenth century, Alonso de Mudarra, canon of the cathedral of Seville, as the instrument on which to play his transcriptions of madrigal settings of several amorous poems of Petrarch and Sannazzaro, including the latter's celebrated sonnet "O gelosia, d'amanti orribil freno..." and the beginning of Eclogue II of *Arcadia*, "I tene allombra degli ameni faggi..."[21] To be noted is that Marsilio Ficino, whose Neoplatonic views on love are frequently echoed in *Diana*, believed that music of plucked instruments was for the soul what medicine was for the body. In his *De vita sana* he prescribed quiet and harmonious music for voice and the cithern whenever the soul is out of tune and troubled by melancholy: "Mercurius, Pythagoras, Plato iubent dissonantem animan vel moerentem cithara cantuque tam constanti quam concinno componere simul atque erigere."[22] Ficino himself was fond of singing and improvising to the accompaniment of his cithern in the circle of the Platonic academy of Florence.

In addition, Castiglione used the expressions "cantare all viola" (singing to the accompaniment of the viola) and "cantare alla viola per recitare" (singing recitative with the viola).[23] However, since there was not only the "viola da arco," but also the "viola da mano," there is no reason to assume that Castiglione meant the latter.[24] Significantly, however, as Gustave Reese observes, the Renaissance translators of the *Cortegiano* into English, French, and German refer to the lute, while the Spanish translator refers to the "vihuela."[25] In the Renaissance, the noblest instrument par excellence is the viol, notes Edward E. Lowinsky, "and the sweetest music is that produced by the quartet of viols,"[26] just as we see in Montemayor's novel. Not surprisingly, four viols contribute to the representation of "heavenly harmony" in a piece of instrumental program music provided by Corteccia and Striggio for *intermedii* by Giovanni Battista Cini, given between the acts of d'Ambra's *La Cofanaria* (1565), a comedy performed at the marriage of Francesco de' Medici and Joanna of Austria. Significantly, Lowinsky goes on to say that in the sixteenth century keyboard instruments were also termed "harmonious," and of these the harpsichord was particularly admired by singers and instrumentalists. To avoid possible difficulties of coordination, of fragmentation of the musical group,

Montemayor at times adds one or more chordal instruments, a keyboard, a lute or harp, to an otherwise seemingly incomplete ensemble. Celia's serenade, termed a "concierto que parescía una música celestial" (p. 106), includes precisely a harpsichord, as we have noted, as well as three trumpets and a sackbut, an arrangement similar to the sonatas *pian e forte* performed in Venice by Giovanni Gabrieli three years after the publication of *Diana*, sonatas which will be extended in Germany during the seventeenth century in such works as the *turmsonaten* of Johann Pezel (Pezelius).[27]

It is interesting to note that *clavicordio* is rendered in Bartholomew Yong's translation of *Diana* as "virginal," an instrument like the harpsichord, so called because "like a virgin, it sounds with a sweet and tranquil voice."[28] The mention of the harpsichord is particularly significant if we bear in mind that the earliest surviving harpsichord is from 1537, and the earliest known perfect example of one is of 1543, both of Italian origin.[29] The newness of the harpsichord is reflected in the fact that it is only mentioned once in Adolfo Salazar's volume on music in Spanish society up to the end of the sixteenth century, and that sole reference is to Montemayor's *Diana*.[30] Significant, too, is the fact that the harpsichord had just been proclaimed "I[n]stromento perfetto" by Angelo Gardaro in 1549.[31] Despite the glowing characterization of the harpsichord, the first half of the sixteenth century "was a period of comparative sterility in the production of keyboard instruments,"[32] and this makes it all the more interesting that a song in *Diana* is set to music with accompaniment including the harpsichord.

As for the use of the harpsichord, Montemayor probably relied on the seven books containing music for *Orgues, Espinettes et Manicordions* ("Organs, Spinets, and Clavichords"), written early in 1531 by Pierre Attaingnant.[33] These keyboard books probably came into the hands of Charles V, who, like his sisters, had been instructed in playing at the keyboard by the famous organist Harry Bredemers.[34] The books by Pierre Attaingnant suggest the important view that "in

France, as in Italy [and Spain], no marked difference existed between music for organ and for stringed keyboard instruments."[35]

The trumpet, played by three gallants honoring Celia, was an instrument of "central importance"[36] in courtly music of the sixteenth century. It was invariably used for official functions, from coronations, marriages, and baptisms, to tournaments and lighthearted musical entertainment. In France's fourteenth-century poem *Les Echecs Amoureux* we read that such instruments as the trumpet, sackbut and bass lute were a favorite on festive occasions: "On sonnoit les haulz instrumens,/ Qui mieulx aux danses plaisoient / Pour la grant noise qu'ils faisoient."[37] The trumpet mentioned in *Diana* is likely the "trompeta bastarda," also known as the "trompeta española," which has a predominantly artistic usage, in contrast to the "Italian trumpet," mainly used for military music. Sebastián de Covarrubias y Horozco explains the nature of the "trompeta bastarda" as "la que media entre la trompeta que tiene el sonido fuerte y grave, y entre el clarín, que lo tiene delicado y agudo" (*Tesoro de la lengua castellana*, Madrid, 1611, s.v.). Those who played the trumpets at such occasions dressed in the most luxurious and dazzling clothes imaginable,[38] a fact deduced from the description of the opulent clothing with which Don Felix and the gallants around him are dressed, all "ricamente vestidos" (p. 110).

Montemayor arranges instruments properly, as he does in his placing of a sackbut with the trumpets, of which it serves as a low, thus observing the medieval distinction between *haut* and *bas* (loud and soft). As for the sackbut, an early version of the trombone, it too is a courtly instrument, as are the others played in the street scene where Celia is honored. It was an instrument that could be easily adapted to all types of voices and instruments by virtue of the elasticity of its tuning. Because of its flexibility it was an instrument that could readily be used to fit an impromptu piece or song, such as a serenade. Players of the sackbut were prominent among the musicians of chapels and courts of kings;[39]

they were performers with whom Montemayor surely came into frequent contact. Worth noting in terms of the importance given to music in *Diana* is the comment that Celia's serenade, performed with the above-cited instruments and many other "diversidades de instrumentos y vozes muy excelentes" goes on through the night, "se acabó muy cerca del alva" (p. 110).

In addition to employing sonnets and the "canción," Book II also makes use of that primitive lyric form, the "villancico," cultivated with extraordinary predilection by poets and court musicians of the Renaissance.[40] Montemayor's own preference for the more spontaneous expression of traditional lyrical forms is revealed by the Portuguese shepherdess Duarda who tells Armia: "Si tu te enamoras de canciones y te parecen bien sonetos hechos con cuydado de dezir buenas razones, desengáñate que son la cosa de que yo menos gusto recibo y por la que menos me certifico del amor que se me tiene" (p. 290). One of the three villancicos used by Montemayor, "Desdeñado soy de amor" (p. 127), together with its musical setting, are recorded in the magnificent collection of polyphonic music (15th—17th centuries) found in the *Cancionero de Upsala* (Venice, 1556; modern edition, Mexico, 1944, pp. 53 [poem], 33). Despite its well-defined external form, this popular lyrico-musical composition possesses great innate flexibility as illustrated by the authorial comment that Selvagia, "mudando el primero verso a este villancico pastoril antiguo, lo començó a cantar aplicándolo a su propósito, desta manera..." (p. 128).

The villancico's fitness for a solo-choral alternation, and its potential for an indefinite continuation by the simple change of a verse, leads to improvisation and a responsorial. This is reflected in the casual manner in which the first two characters take on its singing, and the way in which Sylvano's singing precipitates the song by Selvagia which, in turn, leads Sireno to follow suit. Sylvano sings the "villancico pastoril antiguo," "Quien te fizo, Juan, pastor...," presented as a "diálogo para cantar" by Lucas Fernández; in three voices, by Badajoz (*Cancionero*, Barbieri, n. 360), and with "vihuela," by Esteban Daza (*El Parnaso*,

Valladolid, 1576). Montemayor even glosses this villancico in his *Cancionero* of Zaragoza, 1561. In *Diana*, however, Sylvano changes the first verse of the poem to begin with "Di, ¿quién te a hecho, pastora...?" (p. 128). Later the learned Arsileo plays and sings another "villancico," "este mote antiguo," with a gloss of his own: "Ven, ventura, ven y dura" (p. 255).

To be noted in this regard is that singers of Montemayor's age sought to animate, vary and embellish a simple melodic line, a practice that continued up to the era of the *bel canto*. One way this goal was achieved was through the employment of the *da capo aria* (in two contrasted parts), closing with a repetition of the first part, the dominant song form of the *opera seria*.[41] The grace, fluidity, and spontaneous vitality that characterize the villancico are so well exploited by the two shepherds and the shepherdess who sing them in *Diana* that even the noble nymphs admire its art (p. 129). In fact, the nymphs themselves play a "villancico a tres" with "sus instrumentos tan suavemente que junto con las divinas vozes no parecieron sino música celestial" (p. 72). Although the music is "celestial," the theme of the song is an earthly concern with the fugacity of human contentment.

The sixteenth century was a period that brought with it a great musical revolution: monody with accompaniment.[42] In Book III an unnamed friend of Belisa provides accompaniment for her famous song "Passava amor su arco desarmado" (p. 151) for which she is applauded by the nymphs (p. 154). Also in Book III, parenthetically, Belisa gives an account of how she fell in love with Arsileo for his "natural" talents as poet, singer, and musician.

Indeed, in *Diana* the endowments of nature are not only physical beauty and brightness of mind, but also a fine sensibility for aesthetic values. It is this last gift of nature that makes the lovers of Montemayor's novel so apt at conveying their amorous sentiments through song and music. Hence, Arsileo is seen as a masculine model of human perfection for having learned at the Academy of Salamanca "lo que a los hombres sube a mayor grado que de hombres" (p. 137), that is, poetry and music. After all, the highest erudition among the Greeks, said Cicero, lay in the songs of their voices and the sounds of their strings.[43] Echoing this view, the shepherds of Montemayor's novel criticize Delio, Diana's husband, as uncouth for not being able to sing and play the instruments. The laudation given Arsileo for his musical talent, and the harsh characterization of Delio for his lack of artistic talent, remind us of Alonso Mudarra's comment that Plutarch praised Epaminondas, prince of Greece, for having played and sung well at a banquet, while criticizing Themistocles as ignorant for not having been able to do the same.[44]

Arsileo is particularly skilled at playing the harp and rebec. It should be remembered that, with few exceptions (e.g. Gonzalo de Berceo's *Duelo de la Virgen*),[45] the harp had been, in the Middle Ages, and was now in the Renaissance, one of a handful of instruments reserved for those of the highest musical education.[46] This fact betrays the novel's level of disguise and its relationship to a courtly context. That an instrument designates the quality of the person who is playing was already common in Italy at the beginning of the sixteenth century,[47] and Montemayor remains consistently conscious of associating the proper instrument with the rank of the person playing it. Arsileo, depicted as an "hombre aficionado a la música" (p. 154), is said to have a voice like Orpheus, which not only "agradava el cielo, estrellas y a la clara Luna [Diana]," (p. 150), but also softened the hearts of all the women who heard him sing.

The comparison of Arsileo to Orpheus (p. 150) may well be an oblique reference to Arsileo as a castrato singer. Orpheus, we recall, was killed by the Maenads, devotees of Dionysus, and after his body was dismembered, his head continued to sing. Referring to a piece played by Arsileo on his rebec, the author comments: "y aviendo tañido un poco con una voz más angélica que de hombre humano, dió principio a esta canción..." (p. 231). The reference to "una voz más angélica que de hombre humano" strengthens the possible characterization of Arsileo as a castrato singer. This is particularly so if we note the way a critic of the eighteenth century writes about a leading castrato of his time, Pauluccio, of Rome: "This eunuch, who was then about nineteen years of age, was indeed the wonder of the world. For besides that his voice was higher than anyone else's, it had all the warblings of a nightingale, but with only this difference, that it was much finer; and did not a man know the contrary, he would believe it impossible such a tone could proceed from the throat of anything that was human."[48]

As a final tribute to the art of the castrati may be cited the opinion of the musical historian Enrico Panzacchi (1840-1904), who, late in the nineteenth century, heard with ecstasy one of the surviving castrati in the papal chapel: "What singing! Imagine a voice that combines the sweetness of the flute, and the animated suavity of the human larynx—a voice which leaps and leaps, lightly and spontaneously, like a lark that flies through the air and is intoxicated with its own flight; and when it seems that the voice has reached the loftiest peaks of altitude, it starts off again, leaping and leaping still with equal lightness and equal spontaneity, without the slightest sign of forcing or the faintest indication of artifice or effort; in a word, a voice that gives the immediate idea of sentiment transmuted into sound, and of the ascension of a soul into the infinite on the wings of that sentiment."[49] The presence in *Diana* of a possible allusion to castrati, "angelic," music may add an important historical and artistic dimension to the novel, heretofore unnoticed, making *Diana* one of the first literary works to allude to that type of voice, which emerged only in the middle of the sixteenth century. Worth noting, in terms of Montemayor's ethnic background and his association with the Spanish and Portuguese courts, is the fact that there is recorded the use of castrati in Portugal, during the reign of Don Sebastian (1557-78). In the sixteenth century these Portuguese eunuchs had apparently been imported from Italy, which in turn got most if indeed not all, its castrati from Spain.[50] The fame of the castrati, often referred to as "songbirds," reached its highest point in the eighteenth century when castrati singers "were discussed, compared, and criticized in fashionable drawingrooms... from Russia to Portugal and from Ireland to the borders of the Ottoman Empire."51

Shepherds often greet the new day with music, and their songs and music entertain them on their journey to and from Felicia's palace. Events at the sophisticated and enchanted palace of the wise lady (Book IV) are not devoid of music either. In accordance with the preference of aristocratic society of the time for stringed instruments in indoor entertainment,52 the nymphs participate in the staged entertainment of the shepherds by singing in a trio, accompanying their songs with a fine arrangement of lute, harp and psaltery, the so-called soft instruments most appropriate for song and dance in the "salas de las damas."53

The lute, by far the most common of the plucked strings in Italy, occupied a central position in *intermedio* ensembles throughout most of the sixteenth century.54 Indeed, it was the universal instrument of the Renaissance, and was played both alone and in the accompaniment of singers. Literature for the lute abounds in reference to pieces of "música acordado" since the fifteenth century *Cancioneros*.55 Already in the high Middle Ages the Flemish theoretician and musician Johannes Tinctoris referred to the popularity of the lute as an instrument which was to be "played in banquets, feasts, dances, and private and public functions."56 The festivities and songs characterizing courtly life in the era of Charles V have been competently discussed by Higinio Anglés, among others, who points out the family predilection for such instruments as the lute and the clavichord.57 Significantly, in terms of its presence in *Diana*, the first books on music for lute had appeared in Italy barely fourteen years before Montemayor's birth.58

Of Persian (or possibly Egyptian) origin, the lute was introduced in Spain by the Arabs. It is often mentioned in conjunction with the "vihuela," with which it has great affinity, and its compositions were easily adapted to polyphonic style.59 Appropriately, we read in *Diana* that the nymphs play in unison "con tan gran concierto y melodía, que los presentes estavan como fuera de sí" (p. 167). Infinitely knowledgeable of polyphonic art, which had been successfully placed at the service of the mass by Giovanni Pierluigi da Palestrina and Orlando Lasso, and had been elevated to the rank of "Ars Nova" by the Catholic Monarchs, Montemayor is one of the first writers to employ it in concert in a novelistic context.[60] Such expressions as "suave música y armonía," "dulce armonía," "concertado canto," "grande concierto y melodía," are all reminiscences of the vocabulary of polyphonic musicians.

The musical taste of high society as well as that of the simple folk coincided, as Adolfo Salazar noted, in the desire for clarity in singing, for voice that could easily be heard, with an accompaniment that would be the least intrusive possible.[61] Particularly suitable for such an accompaniment was not only the lute but also the harp, the other "heavenly instrument," which forms part of the nymphs' sumptuous "consort." As for the psaltery, the instrument played by the third nymph, it is well to point out that, brought to the West by the crusaders, it became in the sixteenth century the preferred household instrument of women.[62] As the psaltery was strung about the neck, it would be a particularly convenient instrument for wandering shepherds to play.

Following the performance of the nymphs they are joined by the gathered shepherds and shepherdess, playing their rebecs and a bagpipe, and together they sing in alternation a long poem about love, fortune, and suffering (pp. 167-170). In a clearly Neoplatonic view, the song combines love and suffering, with the former understood as an alleviation of the latter. Music and song are taken seriously by the characters of *Diana*. Commenting on the musical performance at Felicia's palace, the author remarks: "La sabia Felicia y la pastora Felismena estuvieron muy atentas a la música de las nimphas y pastores y assí mismo a las opiniones que cada uno mostrava tener" (p. 170). The longest musical piece of *Diana* is that provided by the enchanted Orpheus, the distraught singer and musician of Ovid's *Metamorphoses*. He was said either to have invented the lyre, an honor, as we have noted, also attributed to Mercury, or to have received it from Apollo, god of music, medicine, and light. Such was his skill that he was credited with the power of taming wild beasts and moving trees by the excellence of his music. In Montemayor's novel, Orpheus entertains the wayfaring group of shepherds gathered at Felicia's palace, singing and playing not the lyre but the harp. His song is a panegyric to the beauty and virtues of noble Spanish women (pp. 180-190).

The passion-ridden characters of the novel find the "sweet" song and music of the enchanted Orpheus so soothing that it leaves them in a state of awe, oblivious to the uncontrolled emotions that have plagued them up to that point: "La canción del celebrado Orpheo fué tan agradable a los oydos de Felismena y de todos los que la oyan, que assí los tenía suspensos, como si por ninguno dellos uviera passado más de lo que presente tenían" (p. 191). Castiglione, we note, was especially fond of the performance of solo voice with plucked string accompaniment,[63] and echoing that humanist's sensibility, the gathered shepherds and shepherdesses bestow praise on Orpheus' harp-playing (p. 179). In passing, it is worth noting, that, as Orpheus is about to begin to sing and play his "heavenly music," the author comments that the rustics will hear Orpheus singing as when he sang in the "tierra de los Ciconios... cuando Cipariso fué convertido en ciprés y Atis, en pino" (p. 179). In the myth recounted by Ovid, Attis, as a devotee of the earth-goddess Cybele, castrated himself under a pine tree; the reference here may be a further indication that Montemayor thought of the part of Arsileo as sung by a castrato. The comparison of Arsileo to Orpheus has already been noted.

The harp is one of seven instruments associated with Orpheus.[64] The substitution of the harp for the lyre, the most widely-cited Orphic instrument, is first cited in Spain by Iñigo López de Mendoza, the Marquis of Santillana, in his *Deçir que fizo el Marqués de Santillana en loor de la reina de Castilla*: "Caliope se levante / E con la harpa d'Orpheo / Las vuestras virtudes cante..."[65] Juan de Mena, a contemporary of

Santillana, provides another panegyric of the Orphic harp in his *Laberinto de Fortuna*, "Mostrose la harpa que Orfeo tañía / quando al infierno lo traxo el amor,"[66] while Alonso Proaza, famed corrector of *La Celestina*, picks up this characterization of the mythic singer: "La harpa de Orpheo e dulce armonía / Forçaua las piedras a venir a su son / Abríe los palacios del triste Plutón,... / ."[67]

By having Orpheus sing and play in the pastoral context of his novel, Montemayor may well be associated with the development of early opera, which relies heavily on both the Orpheus legend and the pastoral setting. Several years before Montemayor, the Italian humanist Angelo Poliziano chose the subject of Orpheus' tragic love and death for the earliest dramatic production on a classical theme in any modern language. The play, *Orfeo*, produced at Mantua in 1471, is half quasi-opera and half pastoral drama, that singular creation of the Renaissance "in which the Theocritan—Virgilian trappings of Arcadia are blended with romantic themes of love."[68]

Poliziano employs both shepherds and a satyr for dramatic representation, since Orpheus was depicted as close to nature, and since it was a shepherd from whom Eurydice was fleeing when she met her death.[69] The presence in *Diana* of its own lecherous wild men who attempt to destroy the sylvan harmony is a further link of Montemayor's novel with the incipient stages of opera. Toward the end of the sixteenth century the material of the celebrated Thracian musician and hero set against a pastoral background will give rise to "one of the very earliest subjects of real opera,"[70] *Dafne* (1594), and then *L'Euridice* (1600), written by O. Rinuccini with music by Peri and Caccini. The primitive operatic treatment of Orpheus will then be expanded by Monteverdi, whose *Orfeo* (1607) opens up the grander treatment of the story by future poets and dramatists.

In their pastoral solitude shepherds enjoy in blissful peace the pure and lofty delights of music and song, and inspiration to play and sing is pervasive. Arsileo, for example, exhorts Amarílida to play and sing with these words: "Aquí tienes tu çampoña, tañe, canta, pastora, que muy bien lo puedes hacer..." (p. 229). In Book V Arsileo is heard playing the rebec so divinely that "parecía cosa del cielo" (p. 231). While the nymph Polydora goes off to take to Belisa the good news of Arsileo's love for the shepherdess, Arsileo waits for their return in the shade of the alder trees, passing the time by playing his rebec and singing a bouquet of tercets that begin with "ya dan buelta el amor y la fortuna" (pp. 250-52). On her return to the site where she left Arsileo, Polydora, now accompanied by Belisa and the nymphs Cinthia and Dórida, sees the shepherd playing and singing an old ballad "¡Qué tiempos, qué movimientos / qué caminos tan estraños...!" (pp. 255-56). Joined in love by Felicia's miraculous water, Sylvano and Selvagia celebrate union by singing a joyful duet to the tune of the bagpipe played by Diana (p. 267).

So fervent is the characters' attachment to song and music that these become a favorite pastime: "Arsileo... por entretener el tiempo en algo... sacó su rabel y començó a cantar desta manera..." (p. 250). When there is no reason to sing a song, the shepherds do not hesitate to invent one. Asks Sireno: " y tú, Sylvano, toma tu flauta y templemos mi rabel con ella y cantaremos algunos versos; aunque coraçón tan libre como el mío ¿qué podrá cantar que dé contento a quien no le tiene?". To which Sylvano replies: "Para esso yo te daré buen remedio... hagamos cuenta que estamos los dos de la manera que esta pastora nos traya al tiempo que por este prado esparzíamos nuestras quexas" (p. 274). The condition of being disappointed in love is never uncommon, notes Peter Marinelli, "indeed, if the disappointment is not really experienced, Renaissance poets are perfectly capable of inventing an unhappy situation as the basis of their melancholy."[71] Freed of his love for Diana (Book VI), Sireno returns to the spring of the alders that was once witness to his love for the shepherdess, and deliberately plunges into a reflection of the joyous past, consequently feeling lonely, because at all times "la memoria de un buen estado causa soledad al que le a perdido" (p. 269). In solitude he takes up his rebec and sings of memory's cruelty and of his desire to free himself of her bondage: "Passados contentamientos / ¿qué queréis? / dexadme, no me canseys..." (p. 270). Following that song, Sireno and Sylvano sing first a duet and then, singing alternately, another song in praise of Diana. With respect to the technique of the alternating song, it is well to remember that the eclogues of the ancients were sung, alternately, by two groups of singers, and in Virgil's third eclogue we read *Amant alterna Camenae* ("The Muses love the alternating song").[72]

It is well known, remarks Edward Lowinsky, "that a good musician can sit down at the piano and improvise in four voices at once. That means he can think in harmonies. It is less well known that the capacity to think in harmonies had to be acquired and developed at a certain period in history, and that period was the Renaissance."[73] Although Montemayor does not describe any scene of singing which would represent harmony in the technical sense described by Lowinsky, nevertheless he is clearly conscious of *armonia* in the conventional meaning as he has Sireno and Sylvano play their flute and rebec while singing in unison. The harmony produced by the simultaneous conception of the song in two voices is sustained in much of the rest of the poem as the two shepherds continue to sing, now in alternating fashion, each one beginning his part of the song with the last verse sung by the other (pp. 276-277). The song in two voices and the lyrics of one voice taken up by another bring about a unified composition as the same thematic substance penetrates all parts of the song. The thematic unity is complemented by the structural harmony given by the parallel rhythm and meter of the five stanzas. The selection of such adjectives as "manso," and "suave," characteristic of the musical domain of the novel, underscores the impression of harmony sought by the author.

Music in the pastoral is not only designed to tell us something about the characters and their standing in the pleasance, notes Thomas Rosenmeyer, "it also characterizes the poetry as a non-private communication."[74] This explains the contests that follow the lament sung in unison by Sylvano and Sireno. A singing contest may be seen as the "logical conclusion to the tendency at work throughout the genre: the matching of perceptive beings in a nexus of friendship and equality."[75] Music, the constant companion of shepherds, accompanies them to the very end of the novel, where the Portuguese shepherdesses Duarda and Armia sing, as does Danteo, to the accompaniment of an unidentified instrument: "Sospiros, niña lembrança..." (p. 289). Calling an end to wasting any more time on "cosa tan escusada" like the love of Danteo for her, Duarda says to Armia: "Mejor será que se gaste el tiempo en cantar una canción" (p. 285). Like their literary counterparts, these "real" shepherdesses exteriorize their emotions through song (in five quatrains), about the mutability of time and life. Music is also the perfect accompaniment to dining; it turns simple food into a princely meal. Says Duarda to Felismena: "Hermosa pastora, aunque el manjar es de pastoras, la comida es de princesa: ¡qué mal pensaste tú quando aquí venías que avías de comer con música!" (p. 288).

2

Describing the use of musical instruments in one of his plays, Lope de Vega affirms that all the effects, such as surprise, lamentation, love, were expressed in the composition of the music itself.[76] Years before Lope de Vega, Montemayor skillfully employed monody and polyphony with a variety of musical instruments to complement precisely these sentiments in the shepherds and shepherdesses of *Diana*. Grief, in particular, finds its utmost expression through music and song, the best vehicle for communicating and alleviating suffering: "...el mal diziéndose / se passa a menos costa que callándolo / y la tristeza en fin va despidiéndose" (p. 30). Similarly comforted by music is Belisa who, in hearing the music of Arsileo, "tan gran alegría llegó a su coracón que sería imposible sabello dezir..." (p. 256). Here, as in Garcilaso's third eclogue, where art "converts grief into beauty,"[77] music placates grief and makes suffering intelligible.

The singer in *Diana* "is removed from the action-world of the prose, where love is suffered as a 'mal,' and introduced into a realm of noble sadness that heightens the sorrow of love and transmutes it into something to be contemplated, as a thing detached."[78] Music makes sadness "less pungent," converting it into a "dolor gustoso, que puede ser saboreado."[79] This is illustrated by the emphasis placed by Montemayor on the music's quality of "dulzura": "Sacó una çampoña que en el çurrón traía y la començó a tocar tan dulcemente (p. 24)... Pues haviendo oído el dulce canto de Selvagia (p. 66)... El cual entonces començava, al son de una harpa que muy dulcemente tañía (p. 108)... Y los pastores y pastoras... se pusieron a la otra parte con sus rabeles y una çampoña que Selvagia muy dulcemente tañía" (p. 167).

Despite the "sweetness" of music, when Sireno sings of his sorrow it only increases it: "contándolo / se me acrecienta, y más en acordárseme / de quan en vano, ¡ay triste!, estoy llorándolo" (p. 31). Music, then, also serves "para subrayar la melancolía y crear un ambiente propicio al cultivo de la tristeza."[80] The ambivalent nature of music is indicated when Arsileo says that "la música es tanta parte para hazer acrecentar la tristeza del triste como la alegría del que más contento vive" (p. 229). This is confirmed when the same song makes Arsileo sad and Amarílida happy.

To the suffering shepherds and shepherdesses gathered at Felicia's palace music has a soothing and an enchanting effect, echoing the Stoics' belief that music affects the ethos of man, that it can reshape him, or purge him. The psychological effect of music, well known in antiquity, was exemplified by the work of the mythical physician Aesculapius, who "with music cured a madman," and stressed that "many are the marvels worked by this art on the distressed souls."[81]

The miraculous effects ascribed to music by the ancient Greeks, "the legends of Amphion and Orpheus, the stories of

Pythagoras, Plato's beliefs in the... ennobling powers of music, all were constantly in the minds of the Renaissance musicians."[82] The beneficial effects of song and music on the spirit of man were reiterated in the Renaissance, under the influence of the Neoplatonism of Marsilio Ficino, by such respected musicologists as Anríquez de Valderrábano in the Prologue to his *Silva de sirenas* (Valladolid, 1547) and Juan Bermudo in his *Declaración de instrumentos* (Osuna, 1549-1555). Castiglione himself reminds us that music has the power to induce a good new habit of mind and an inclination to virtue, rendering the soul more capable of happiness, just as corporal exercise makes the body more robust.[83] Quite fittingly, Cervantes will write that music "compone los ánimos descompuestos y alivia los trabajos que nacen del espíritu" (*Quijote* I, 28).

In *Diana* the seductive power of harmony is mentioned when Orpheus "començó a tañer en una harpa que en las manos tenía, muy dulcemente, de manera que los que le oyan, estavan tan agenos de sí que a nadie se le acordava de cosa que por el uviesse passado" (p. 179).[84] Orpheus, we will recall, plays and sings in honor of virtuous Spanish women, whose conduct is to be emulated by the visitors to Felicia's palace. Orpheus demonstrates the hypnotic power of music, when his song keeps the wayfaring shepherds "suspensos como si por ninguno d'ellos uviera passado más de lo que presente tenían" (p. 191). The mesmerizing effect of music is not reserved to the sound of the courtly harp played by Orpheus; it is also produced by the rustic bagpipe played by Sireno: "tan dulcemente que el valle, el monte, el río, las aves enamoradas y aun las fieras de aquel espeso bosque quedaron suspensos" (p. 24). Music thus also provides a new dimension of life to nature, the great paradigm of the novel.

Music, furthermore, plays the ancillary role of removing the reader from the monotony of the pastoral lament to savor momentarily the beauty of the verses: "The element of play-acting suggested by the singing breaks the spell of empathy and helps us to disregard the suffering so as to enjoy the beauty more."[85] Solos, duets, and short instrumental interludes lend variety and entertainment to the novel.

Singing is witnessed, and it is also heard from afar: "...los nuevos enamorados y el descuydado Sireno... antes que llegasen a la fuente de los alisos, oyeron una voz de una pastora que dulcemente cantava" (p. 240). In this case, the voice turns out to be that of Diana, who provides a much needed lyrical interlude to break up the narration about Arsileo and Belisa. The ballad sung by Diana serves, further, as a postponement of the reunion of Arsileo and Belisa, thus adding to the suspense of their story.

Music also regulates plot development and aids in shifting the direction of the narrative. When the Portuguese shepherdesses are about to inquire into the reason for Felismena's tears (the answer to which would have given further prominence to the Felismena-Felix story), a shepherd's voice is heard in the background, and with it there is a change of scene: "Y queriéndole pedir la causa, se lo estorvó la voz de un pastor, que muy dulcemente, al son de un rabel cantava, el qual fue luego conocido de las dos pastoras porque aquel era el pastor Danteo por quien Armia terciava con la graciosa Duarda" (p. 288). Danteo's intercalated song, and the ensuing dialogue among Duarda, Armia and Felismena, shed light on the story of the Portuguese shepherds, while putting off the reappearance of Felix.

Also affecting plot is Arsenio's praise of his son Arsileo's singing and playing (p. 146). His action is significant in terms of plot development for, as Belisa tells us, it was intended to "dar ocasión a los que con él estavan le rogassen que embiasse por una harpa a casa y que allí tañesse y cantasse porque estava en parte que yo por fuerça avía de gozar de la música" (p. 147). The reason for the father's staged performance is revealing: "Quando yo oy a Arsileo y sentí la melodía con que tañía, la soberana gracia con que cantava, luego estuve al cabo de lo que podía ser, entendiendo que su padre me quería dar música y enamorarme con las gracias del hijo" (p. 147). Parenthetically, the realization that Arsenio wanted Belisa to fall in love with him to the sound of his son's music leads Belisa to make the prophetic comment that no one should dare to make his lady fall in love with him by means of another's charms, "porque algunas vezes, suele acontecer enamorarse más la dama del que tiene la gracia, que del que se aprovecha della, no siendo suya" (p. 147).

3

In addition to song and instrumental music, *Diana* possesses also a musical tone in its very language, as Menéndez y Pelayo perceived early in the history of criticism of *Diana*: "La prosa de Montemayor... es tersa, suave, melódica, expresiva, más musical que pintoresca..."[86] Understandably, Felismena says to the Portuguese shepherdess Duarda: "No avría en el mundo, graciosa pastora, música más agradable para mí que vuestra vista y conversación" (p. 288). Montemayor's descriptions of the landscape, particularly, create "a mild, soft, musical atmosphere."[87] The lyrical character of the prose evokes a sort of "recitar cantando," an expression coined by the Roman playright Emilio dei Cavalieri in his *La rappresentazione* (1600), as a work completely set to song and music, in contrast to earlier drama in which music had only an accessory role.[88]

As is common in the pastoral genre, Montemayor makes greater use of prenominal attributive adjectives than any other type of adjective, thus stressing an affective rather than a contrastive or distinguishing quality:[89] "caudaloso río"... "olvidado Sireno"... "triste vida"... "verdes y deleitosos prados" (p. 9), "clara fuente" ... "altos y verdes alisos" (p. 11). The prime characteristic of these vocative epithets and other proposed adjectives is as Emileo Náñez has noted, "su señalada intención estética... Es decir en este orden expresivo es más importante cómo se comunica una noticia que la noticia en sí... con lo que se completa esa curva rítmico—melódica, de gran efecto fonético en una lectura en voz alta."[90] The fact that the preposed adjective is supposed to express an assumed or inherent rather than a distinguishing attribute[91] may be linked to the Platonic aesthetic[92] and ideological background of *Diana*. The profusion of prenominal adjectives thus suggests the ideal portrayed in the work as well as the reality so keenly sought by the author. It has been said that in the pastoral play *Aminta*, by the Italian humanist Torquato Tasso, "words are hovering on the edge of song at every moment; every phrase is filled with the unheard music which Tasso himself called 'the sweetness and, so to speak, the soul of poetry'".[93] The same linguistic musicality pervades the prose and verses of *Diana*.

Chapter II

La Diana and the Visual Arts

Much of the novel's action takes place by the banks of the river Esla, "hermosa ribera," with a "fuente de alisos" (spring of the alder trees), close to a thick woodland (pp. 9-10). [1] This and other parts of the setting are described pictorially with light and color: "rayos del sol" (p. 241); "cristalinas aguas" (p. 63); "verde y ameníssimo prado" (p. 280); architectonically, by injecting dimensions and perspective: "campo [de] doze millas" (p. 280); "hondo valle" (p. 64); "alta sierra" (p. 280); poetically (with references to the sky and infinite space): "alto cielo," "[estrella del] norte" (p. 192); "dorado Phebo" (p. 134); "clara luna" (pp. 150, 161). Nature is perceived not only with all its particular detail of color but also of scent (e.g. "olorosas flores," p. 28); and shepherds enjoy the scent of jasmine, (p. 191) honeysuckle (p. 191) and roses (p. 282). Adjectives bring out the picture of nature at its best: "fresca," "dorada," "suave," "bella;" clear images of the external world as were recorded on canvas by such Renaissance artists as Leonardo da Vinci and Albrecht Dürer, both of whom stressed the supremacy of nature as a source of beauty and artistic inspiration.[2]

The pastoral setting of *Diana* exudes abundance, variety and opulence. A summary of the flora in *Diana* shows that the author mentions grasses and herbs, bushes, shrubs, a number of different kinds of trees, and several flowers. Shepherds move amidst alders (p. 281), beeches and elms (p. 66); willows (pp. 25, 130, 281), ilexes (p. 229) and oaks (pp. 73, 282); ash trees (pp. 33, 282) and laurels (pp. 71, 93, 178, 191, 269, 270). The characters cross flax fields (p. 282), climb mulberry trees (pp. 158, 235), pass by wild olive (p. 281) and cypress trees

(p. 164), and under garlands of ivy (pp. 41, 282) and grape arbors (pp. 191, 203).

In *Diana*, the "green cabinet," as Thomas G. Rosenmeyer refers to the pastoral setting,[3] harbors a varied fauna as well. In addition to countless references to sheep, there are also mentions of goats (pp. 52, 282, 291), cattle (pp. 150, 155, 292) and horses (pp. 105, 110, 294, 299), all of which are vital components of the novel's bucolic setting. As Sireno leaves the village on his way to the alder spring he comes to the campestral setting that was once witness to his love for Diana and sees her dogs, who fawn upon him to show their delight at seeing him (p. 269). Shepherds participate in hunting (of deer, presumably, p. 33) and they see wolves seeking out their prey (p. 65), all of which emphasises the fact that in pastoral literature, unlike the fable or the Gothic tale, animals are true animals.[4] The word "bucolic," so often applied to the setting of *Diana*, is itself highly suggestive. It derives from the Greek *boukolos*, a keeper of cattle as opposed to a shepherd or goatherd, and represents an enhancement of the social status of the figures of pastoral poetry. The role of shepherd and neatherd is illustrated in a sixteenth-century woodcut from Spenser's "The Shepheard's Calendar, 1579."[5]

Like Theocritus, Montemayor pays relatively little attention to birds in spite of what is for him, as for the classical poet, "an acute awareness of the beauty of their song. When they occur, they are built into the scenery, rather than playing a part as other animals do."[6] Thus we have, for example, a reference to "el ave que lleva el viento" (p. 14). In the few instances where they are mentioned (e.g. Arsenio's letter), birds, like fish, are extolled for the freedom they enjoy, a freedom for which, says Arsenio, "daré yo mi libertad" (p. 141). In addition to references to unspecified birds (pp. 88, 134), there are a few concrete mentions of an owl (p. 278), nightingales (pp. 75, 163) and, significantly, a singing insect, the cicada (p. 278).

In a way that reminds us of the expressive account of nature found in Homer (*Odyssey* V, 63-74) and Virgil (*Aeneid* I, 159-168), the spectacle of natural elements in *Diana* suggests that nature in Montemayor's novel, as in the painting of the time, is ingeniously sketched to convey a sense of choreographic beauty, peace, and harmony. The *locus amoenus* is given a further stroke of art with frequent references to the shade of the alder trees, to which shepherds and shepherdesses regularly go to commiserate with each other in their suffering. A similar preference for the somber and shady setting is also seen in Garcilaso's third eclogue where in one spot trees are so thickly entwined with ivy that the sun cannot shine through the foliage. It does not surprise us, therefore, that in her examination of the adjectives of color present in this eclogue Margot Arce should have noted only one mention of blue.[7] The shepherds' affinity to the shade of the alders complements the pictorial vogue in the Renaissance for shade used daringly on canvas for the first time by Leonardo da Vinci, "el primero que hizo osadamente la sombra."[8]

The relationship of *Diana* to the pictorial trends of the Renaissance links Montemayor to the humanists' adherence to the Horatian principle of *ut pictura poesis*—as in painting so in poetry. This view was expounded in the middle of the sixteenth century by Ludovico Dolce who proclaimed that not only poets, but all writers are painters; that poetry, history, and in short, every composition of learned men is painting.[9] The expressive movement in painting, stressed by such theorists as Leon Battista Alberti[10] and Giovanni Paolo Lomazzo,[11] who reminded their contemporaries of the importance of gesture and facial expression as vital means of conveying human emotion, is repeatedly captured in *Diana*. To cite just a few examples, Felix claps Valerio (Felismena in disguise) on the shoulder (p. 116); Sylvano pulls Selvagia's arm (p. 227); smiling, Felicia whispers to Felismena (p. 170); Belisa is seen "bolviendo los ojos al cielo, con una ansia que parecía que el coraçón se le arrancava" (p. 146); in one of their final dialogues with Diana, the shepherds Sireno and Sylvano, we are told, "respondieron con otras palabras y otros movimientos de rostro, de lo que le respondían a lo que ella solía preguntalles" (p. 245). Relating Montemayor's visual expression to the pictorial arts it is well to point out that

Leonardo, possible remembering Quintilian, advises the painter to learn the fine points of expressive movement from the dumb, whose only speech is gesture.[12] By the same token, the German dramatist and critic Gotthold Lessing in his *Laokoön* (1766) would later make the visual imagination the cornerstone of good poetry, declaring that "the poet should always paint."[13]

In poetry, as in painting, Renaissance critics insisted on decorum, defined by Leonardo as "appropriateness of gesture, dress and locality."[14] Montemayor's characterization of Don Felix as a knight opulently dressed (e.g. "faxas de terciopelo amarillo... calças de terciopelo blanco, recamadas... jubón de raso blanco, recamado de oro" (p. 111), in a courtly setting, serenading his beloved Celia at the court of Augusta Caesarina, reflects an acute awareness of artistic propriety. This is noted also in the description of the actions of the wealthy landlord Arsenio and his educated son Arsileo, as well as in the portrayal of Lady Felicia, ("vestida de raso negro," p. 163), an urbane figure, admired for the "gravedad y arte de su persona" p. 163), who gives lessons on Neoplatonic love doctrine with the erudite words of an actual philosopher, Leone Ebreo, in a palace containing the best of a materially rich civilization: "chapiletes de las columnas doradas ... casa de reluciente jaspe ... mesas de fino cedro ..." (pp. 173-179).

In *Diana* the shepherd Sireno comes to the setting of the alders from the mountains of León, with a "vestido tan áspero como su ventura [y] un cayado en la mano" (p. 10). Sireno's rugged clothing evokes an image of the coarse clothes worn by shepherds in Giorgione's *Adoration of the Shepherds* (National Gallery of Art, Washington, D.C.). The shepherd's crook, so often mentioned in *Diana* (e.g. pp. 10, 27, 30) is also carried by the herdsmen represented in the visual arts from the oldest vase paintings of Greece where Pan, the god of Arcadia, clad in skins is carrying a *lagóbolon*, (the Greek equivalent of the shepherd's crook),[15] to Medieval frescoes and Renaissance medals. Engraved on one such medal, attributed to Cristoforo Caradosso Foppa (1475- c. 1527), is a shepherd with crook and a meager cloak seated under a tree, with a dog at his feet pointing with right hand up a path along which sheep descend from an enclosure through an arched gateway.[16] The dog brings to mind the scene when Sireno is greeted by Diana's dogs which "meneando las colas y baxando los pescueços que de agudas puntas de azero estavan rodeados, se le echaron a los pies" (p. 269). The arched gateway is a vivid reminder of the proximity of the pastoral setting to an urban center, as we see in *Diana* where Felismena speaks to the Portuguese rustics Danteo, Duarda, and Armia, with Coimbra looming majestically in the background (pp. 286-288).

The grieving tone of the novel is established at the beginning of Book I, which proclaims the shepherds' principal enemies, love, fortune and time: "Baxaba de las montañas de León el olvidado Sireno a quien Amor, la fortuna, el tiempo, tratavan de manera que del menor mal que en tan triste vida padecía, no se esperava menos que perdella" (p. 9). It has been widely noted that novelistic action in *Diana* is shaped to a large extent on the power of fortune. In the first part of the novel fortune casts down all the important characters—Sylvano, Sireno, Diana, Selvagia, Felismena, Belisa. In the second part, fortune lifts them all up, with the exception of Diana whose transgression of the canons of loyalty plunge her into a permanent state of unhappiness, fulfilling the two basic functions of fortune, as given by Horace, that of lifting the dejected and of subduing the vain and proud.[17] The importance of fortune in *Diana* may be gauged by the 105 mentions of fortune, as a deity who capriciously guides shepherd's lives, and fifteen references to *hado* or *hados*.[18] Fortune's universality is perceived by the fact that even the savages who attack nymphs are subject to fortune: "...no era justo que la fortuna hiziesse tan grande agravio a nuestros cativos coraçones como era dilatalles tanto su remedio" (p. 88).

Fortune, like love, brings suffering. Both are the "autores de trabajos y sinrazones" (p. 167). Since love is not based on reason, its success or failure depends on fortune (p. 169), a powerful force against which rail discontented shepherds and shepherdesses alike. The indifference and hostility of fortune represented by its eternal *mudança* leads to much of the novel's pastoral lament. "No se suffría menos sino venir de un extremo a otro," cries out Sireno, "que mal contado le sería a la fortuna dexar de hazer comigo lo que con todos haze" (p. 15). Fortune's fickle nature "en un momento / corta la rayz del alegría" (p. 35), as Selvagia points out, adding "fortuna me robó mi gloria" (p. 65). Fortune's cruelty is stressed by Sireno who reminds Slyvano and Selvagia, newly joined in love, of fortune's instability (p. 239).

Invariably, it is fortune that is to be blamed for leading lovers into unresolvable and painful situations: "Caer de un buen estado / es una grave pena y importuna, / mas no es amor culpado / la culpa es de fortuna / que no sabe exceptar persona alguna" (p. 169). The unhappiness brought on by love seems to have its ultimate roots in fate. The words that Alanio pronounces to Ysmenia may well refer to the entire cast of unfortunate shepherds: "¿Qué hado, Ysmenia, es este que te obliga / a amar do no es possible ser amada?" (p. 54). In accordance with abundant examples that show a greater propensity for adverse fortune to act upon those who are already suffering,[19] fortune in *Diana* seems to be particularly harsh toward those who love most genuinely. With a distinct tone of pessimism, Sylvano speaks to Selvagia in this way: "No sin grandíssima compassión se deve considerar, hermosa Selvagia, la diversidad de tantos y tan desusados infortunios como suceden a los tristes que queremos bien" (p. 68). Fortune is particularly harsh to Belisa, another exemplary lover. "Pues viviendo yo con todo el contentamiento del mundo, viéndome tan de veras amada de Arsileo, a quien yo tanto quería, parece que la fortuna determinó de dar fin a mis amores con el más desdichado sucesso que jamás en ello se ha visto" (p. 157).

In her dillusionment, Selvagia blames cruel fortune for her suffering, and says that the only cure will be throwing "un clavo al exe de la rueda" (p. 36), and Sylvano feels persecuted by "enbidiosa fortuna" (p. 151). Yet little, if anything, can be done against the "golpes de la fortuna" (p. 125). Selvagia accuses fortune of being the cause of her separation from a valley where all things used to bring her joy: "¿o qué fortuna me apartó de un valle / que toda cosa en él me dava gloria?" (p. 65).

Referred to as "the most time-conscious author of early Spanish literature,"[20] Montemayor populates a bucolic world with human types who are keenly aware of the influence of the past, and the brevity of a present that plunges restlessly into the future. Not suprisingly, at least one critic has described *Diana* "as a study in the impermanence of human attachments."[21] This explains the presence of only sparse and fleeting references to rare moments of amorous happiness in the life of shepherds (e.g. 228, 238, 260), and virtually all of these are found in the parts following the events in Felicia's palace. Temporal consciousness and the brevity of amorous passion, so eloquently apprehended in *Diana*, imbue the novel with a distinctly human reality and an essential morality. Against the poetic belief of the lover that his passion is a timeless experience, Montemayor projects the lives of Sireno, Sylvano, Diana and Selvagia to illustrate the lesson that love, like all other human experiences, is transitory.

The unstable nature of love, fortune, and time, is captured in an engraving entitled *Death surprising a woman* by Agostino Veneziano de' Musi (c. 1490—c. 1540). The picture shows the figure of Death with an hourglass, a wheel of Fortune and a woman looking in the mirror.[22] Fortune's wheel and Fortune personified are also depicted on an unidentified Venetian medal of the first quarter of the sixteenth century. Drifting over the sea on a broken wheel, Fortune is represented nude with long forelock blowing foward and a fluttering scarf passing behind her back.[23]

De' Musi's representation of a woman looking in the mirror invites us to think further of Sireno's object of love, the vain Diana. Diana's vanity is clearly portrayed in the scene of Book I where Sylvano recounts how in the early relationship between Sireno and Diana he had seen her combing her hair in front of a mirror which was held by Sireno (p. 21). As Sireno contemplates Diana, she, rather than returning the lover's gaze, contemplates her own image.24 The scene is rich in allegorical and moral significance. Reflected in the mirror the beautiful shepherdess can only see vainglory, transience and death, as does the woman in Titian's painting *Young Woman Doing Her Hair*, probably executed between 1512 and 1515,25 a picture conceivably known to Montemayor.

The mirror, notes Erwin Panofsky, "was the standard attribute not only of Prudence and Truth but also of Vanity, in the sense of being inordinately pleased with oneself as well as in the more terrible sense of the Preacher's 'Vanity of vanities; all is Vanity'; and it is not surprising that in the Renaissance it came to be associated with death."26 Diana's repeated enchantment with the mirror "en que de quando en quando [la pastora] se mirava" (p. 21) at the expense of looking at Sireno is an echo of the situation found in the painting in which the man "is steeped so deep in a shadow... that, in spite of his presence, the woman seems to be alone with her thoughts."27 In *Diana*, the shepherdess' action of looking at the mirror betrays the tenuous relationship between Diana and Sireno even in their early days together, thus anticipating her inconstancy, while underscoring the finality of all human endeavors, a lesson vividly evoked by Titian's heroine, who seems to be addressing her beholder with what seems to be a "You may well be what we are now; but soon / Both you and we will cease to love and live."28 This message is also quite appropriate for Montemayor's novel, where Diana and Sireno will indeed cease to love—she, her husband, Delio; he, Diana, and without love both will fade into oblivion. Regarding Diana's use of the mirror, it is well to remember, too, that in Dante's allegorical journey through purgatory, Virgil explains why the souls there are "thin" by giving an example from mythology and an analogy based on form and its image in a mirror (*Purgatory*, XXV, 22-27). Shakespeare's sonnet No. 77 gives a stark reminder of the role of the mirror in these terms "thy glass will show thee how thy beauties wear." A biographer of the famed sculptor Gian Lorenzo Bernini reminds us, further, that in a mirror designed by Bernini and once owned by Queen Christina of Sweden, the glass is being uncovered by Time himself in order to "reveal... the decay of the viewer's beauty and youth."[29]

Diana has thus been guilty of passion in the form of narcissism, anticipating with that the sort of lust which Rousseau tried to channel back into the pastoral spectrum.[30] It is possible that in such characterization of Diana, Montemayor wished to convey his concern with the moral dangers of idleness, a lesson clearly perceived also in a reference to the deceitful Ysmenia combing her golden hair by a brook (p. 52). We will recall, for example that Felix is sent to the court of the great Princess Augusta Cesarina by his father saying, albeit schemingly, that "no era justo que un cavallero moço y de linaje tan principal, gastasse la mocedad en casa de su padre, donde no se podían aprender sino los vicios de que la ociosidad es maestra" (p. 104).

The sensual portrayal that is sometimes achieved by the novelist's detailed descriptions of the shepherdesses' bodies (e.g. Belisa's "blanco pecho," "gracioso bulto," "cabellos ruvios," "blanco pie descalço," (p. 132), finds a parallel in the paintings of a Parma painter by the name of Antonio Allegri known as Correggio (1494-1534). His particular achievement lies in the intelligent, delicate and suggestive strokes with which he creates the human hand, a part of the body that in *Diana* betrays the aristocratic background of some of its characters, such as Ysmenia, for example, whose "hermosa y delicada mano" (p. 49) is attentively admired by Selvagia.

Selvagia's account of how Ysmenia, who claims to be a man, disguises herself as a woman in order to enter the Temple of Minerva, was probably inspired by a classical novelette about a handsome young Athenian, Hymenaeus, who cloaked himself in female attire to participate in sacred festivals with his loved one.[31] The theme is represented by Nicolas Poussin in a large painting called *A Floral Offering to Hymen, God of Marriage*. Now in the São Paolo Museum in Brazil, this work of art is intelligently examined by Walter Friedlaender,[32] and from his observations one can distill some revealing parallels between it and the episode found in *Diana*. In the day preceding the sacred activities in the temple, the shepherdesses of *Diana*, dressed "de los mejores [paños] que teníamos" (p. 41), delight themselves in the company of some shepherds by singing and playing their musical instruments while other shepherds indulge in a variety of competitive games (p. 41). In the painting some matrons and virgins of Athens, clad in wide colorful chitons and wearing on their heads either headcloths, flowers or floral wreaths, kneel in adoration of the god Pan, while others dance solemnly to the music of a lyre and a double flute.

Once inside the novel's Temple of Minerva, attention is drawn to one shepherdess in particular, Ysmenia, who, sitting next to Selvagia, is staring silently and intensely into her eyes (p. 42). Upon removing her headdress, Selvagia recounts, Ysmenia betrays a presence and countenance "un poco varonil" (p. 44). In the painting one figure at the extreme right stands motionless and apart from the others and is without a headcloth. What is more revealing is that she, unlike the other maidens, wears sandals which are clearly those of a man.

It has been rightly pointed out that a characteristic of Poussin is not to generalize, "but to chose a precise literary subject and, on the basis of the narrative, to depict a whole spectacle, going far beyond the simple telling of the story."[33] The intricate tale of Selvagia recounted with such breadth, vividness and profusion of detail decidedly suggests that long before the French painter exhibited his art on canvas Montemayor had already brought to view an intrepid array of eye-cathing situations to deepen and enrich the narration of a particular event.

Following Selvagia's story, she, along with the shepherds Sireno, Sylvano, and the three nymphs whom they met in Book II, come upon a band of wild men, three savages "de extraña grandeza y fealdad" (p. 87). At that point the charming and peaceful setting of the pastoral is suddenly disrupted by the attack of the wild men on the nymphs whom they attempt to ravish. Only the fortuitous intervention of a noblewoman dressed as a huntress, Felismana, who kills the wild men, saves the nymphs. In continuation of the story of Hymenaeus there is a similar account of how, at one of the sacred festivals, noblewomen and beloved maidens are suprised by corsairs and abducted into slavery. There Hymenaeus kills the pirates and liberates the women. Poussin did not execute a pianting to portray this part of the Hymenaeus legend, but he does introduce a weird spectacle of violence into a pastoral setting, in his *Rape of Europa*. In this and various other compositions of Poussin (e.g. *Birth of Bacchus, Apollo and Daphne*) "elements of despair, of menacing death, unexpectedly appear in stories of joy, fertility, or idyllic peace."[34] Pictorial versions of *Apollo and Daphne* and the *Rape of Europa* by artists preceding Montemayor, such as Antonio Pollaiuolo (1447-1496), Francesco di Giorgio (1439-1502), and Albrecht Dürer convey the same intrusion of violence in a pastoral setting.

"The shepherd...seems to possess the greatest of all luxuries, the one most indispensable to art: leisure."[35] It has been pointed out above that on the day prior to entering the sacred Temple of Minerva the pastoral community cited in Montemayor's novel take part in festivities that include singing and playing (p. 41) and, later in the novel, shepherds and shepherdesses participate in dancing as well. The gathering of shepherds and shepherdesses in what seems a rustic picnic for the sake of eating and drinking in the country, remindful of the last section of Theocritus's *Idyll* 7[36] and of Horace's *Odes* 3.18, finds a parallel in the open-air party depicted in Renaissance painting by Giorgione and Bellini.

As for singing, it is an intrinsic part of shepherds' life; shepherds were, after all, "musical creatures"[37] by nature. As has been noted, solitude invites shepherds to sing about the toils and hardships of their work, to chant about the beauty of nature or utter hymns about people dear to them. The rich collection of traditional lyric poetry gathered by Dámaso Alonso and José Manuel Blecua offer ample examples of pastoral poems that have a distinct relationship to the reality of medieval and Renaissance pastoral life.[38] López Estrada stresses the point that the reader of the time did not look upon pastoral works as solely the product of literary sources of antiquity, but rather as an echo of a lexicon, of shepherds and their songs and musical instruments, of rivers, mountains, and valleys well known to them.[39] When the shepherds are not speaking of love or praising the beauty of their women, they should indulge, Sylvano tells us, in those activities "de que los pastores nos preciamos, como son tañer, luchar, jugar al cayado, baylar con las moças el domingo" (p. 30). A scene of shepherds with bagpipes and flute is beautifully rendered in an anonymous woodcut of 1491,[40] and a picnic style Flemish scene with a shepherd playing bagpipes is seen in Pieter Bruegel's *Peasants' Dance* (Kunsthistorisches Museum, Vienna), a painting produced in the years of Montemayor's travels to the Netherlands. A dancing shepherd is also reproduced in a detail of a Nativity scene by the so-called Astorga Master (Madrid, Lázaro Collection),[41] a scene that would have been particularly admired by Montemayor who produced three pastoral *autos* for presentation before Prince Philip during the Christmas festivities of 1547.[42]

Pastoral talent in these endeavors is such that we can well say of *Diana*'s shepherds what has been noted of Góngora's peasants in the *Soledades*, that their skill at singing, dancing, and playing musical instruments shows "admirable artifice," and a distinct "degree of culture and civilization."[43] It is all part of the novel's "sympathetic realism" that softens rural coarseness to make country life palatable to urban society.[44] The varied merry-making described by Sylvano's words is reminiscent of the ingenuity of Golden Age Spaniards to satisfy their craving for any sort of rejoicing.[45] Dance, particularly, was a "national passion"[46] of the time, and reflecting this passion Cervantes wrote in one of his plays: "No hay mujer española que no salga del vientre de su madre bayledora."[47] With dancing, to borrow an expression of Michael Squires, "we smell the fragrance of leisure and fesivity,"48 which echoes not only pastoral life but also courtly pastime.

In the Spanish Renaissance "people danced everywhere, and everyone danced." At the court and in aristocratic circles, records the literary historian, Marcelin Defourneaux, "the pavan, the branle, and the allemande were danced to the sound of instruments; measured and formal, by the grandees and their ladies."49 For this, Sylvano's description of shepherds' pastime is significant in terms of what it reveals. In Castiglione's *Courtier* we are told that pastoral entertainments are a "calculated strategy to reveal the cavalier in the most favorable light. Though in his own person the knight may not with propriety dance or wrestle with peasants, in a masquerade he can freely enact his natural grace... because masquerading carries with it a certain freedom and license, which among other things enables one to chose the role in which he feels most able...and to show a certain nonchalance in what does not matter: all of which adds much charm; as for a youth to dress as an old man, yet in loose attire so as to be able to show his vigor; or for a cavalier to dress as a rustic shepherd, or in some other costume, but astride a perfect horse and gracefully attired in character."50 Thus, despite its artifice and idealization of life, the pastoral novel is not as false as it seems. *Diana*, in particular, is an authentic expression of Renaissance idealism, exalting the values of the individual and of human personality, while delving into the inner make-up of man.

Furthermore, the stage for some of those fêtes referred to above by Defourneaux were not without allegorical figures (e.g. knights of the sea, moon, stars and death, the latter knight dressed in black velvet), and magic flasks, music and dance. Felicia, we will remember, appears clothed in black velvet, and she too makes use of a miraculous flask. In addition, entertainment in her palace includes music and song. Besides depicting shepherds in conventional musical groupings in which they play rustic instruments, the evening fête in Felicia's palace represents them with the nymphs in sumptuous concerts which include lutes, harps, psaltery and other "heavenly instruments," a fact betraying the novel's level of disguise and its courtly context. Like several sixteenth-century booklets dealing with Italian court entertainment which list in detail the instruments that accompanied the singers of specific compositions,[51] this scene in *Diana* makes specific reference to the evening's musical arrangements, all carried, with the exception of one bagpipe, with the so-called "low sounding instruments," which are most appropriate for song and dance in the "salas de las damas".[52] The rebec, an instrument much cultivated in the fifteenth century, but virtually absent from the Florentine *intermedii* of the sixteenth century,[53] appears in *Diana* with vigor, and is also present at the festivity in Felicia's palace, suggestive of its importance in the courtly musical life of sixteenth-century Spain. As we noted, of the twenty-three instruments listed in the inventory of musical instruments in the royal orchestra of Charles V and Philip II,[54] where Montemayor served as singer and musician, twelve are mentioned in *Diana* and four are played by the shepherds and nymphs in Felicia's palace. Here, as in the episodes related to Felismena's life at court, music takes on a function of social realism that reminds us of the early popular drama (e.g. Francesco Cherea, *Egloga pastoral*, 1508; Angelo Beolco, *Pastorale*, 1520).

Shepherds, or courtly figures in disguise, the characters of *Diana* play a variety of wind and string instruments, some of them the latest musical inventions of the Renaissance, including the "vihuela da corda" and the clavichord. Part of *Diana*'s collection of instruments is reflected pictorically in an anonymous work of the sixteenth century, *Group of Musicians*, showing some of the most fashionable courtly instruments of the time, left to right: viola da gamba, flute, lute, viola, coronet, harp, trumpet, krumm or crooked horn, spinet (also known as virginal or clavichord).[55] A light model of the clavichord, and the one probably carried by the characters serenading Celia, is one of the type created by Domenico da Pesaro (Venice, 1543), now held in the Art History Museum of Vienna.[56] In Felicia's palace (p. 179), Orpheus probably plays a type of harp akin to a so-called "Irish harp," which came into use during the second half of the thirteenth century. It was a "far heavier instrument" than the earlier versions "with a massive sound box, increasing greatly in width towards the bass, with a strongly arched neck and a heavily curved fore-pilllar... It is first found in the carvings of the Angel Choir at the Lincoln Cathedral, which date from *c.* 1270."[57] Depicted in these carvings is King David with an Irish harp having brays in the belly. "These are L-shaped pegs which not only pin the strings into the belly but whose horizontal arm touches the string lightly and produces a buzzing sound which increases the volume considerably and helps the sound to sustain,"[58] a particularly desirable feature for the Song of Orpheus. A good example of the "Irish harp" is retained at Trinity College, Dublin.[59]

Examples of the lyre and rebec, often used by characters of *Diana*, are shown in Nicholas Bessaraboff's *Ancient European Musical Instruments* (Boston: Published for the Musuem of Fine Arts by Harvard University Press, 1941), Plate X. There is also an expressive figure of an angel playing a rebec in a fresco in Santa Maria in Aracoeli (Rome) executed by Pinturicchio (1454-1513).[60] Other instruments played in *Diana* include sackbuts, and cornets[61] shown in Montagu's collection of Renaissance instruments, and depicted pictorally by J. Aman's *Consort of gentlemen, one playing the sackbut*.[62]

Despite their music, singing and dancing, the shepherds and shepherdesses of *Diana*, disillusioned and distraught by amorous torment, wander aimlessly in the confused solitude of their *locus amoenus* until rescued from their meandering existence by three nymphs, Polydora, Cynthia and Dórida, all priestesses of the wise Lady Felicia. The nymphs form a triad bearing a possible significance often associated with the Three graces as symbols of Friendship and Concord. Individually, the nymphs also betray traits invested on each of the Three Graces *Castitas-Pulchritudo-Amor*, so identified in a medal made by Niccolò Fiorentino on the occasion of the marriage of Giovanna degli Albizzi to Pico della Mirandola's pupil, Lorenzo

Tornabouni. In addition to this medal, Fiorentino produced another medal depicting the three graces as *Fortitudo, Pulchritudo,* and *Amor*.[63] Parenthetically, Diana's nymphs bring to mind the nymphlike figures that appear in Dante's *Divine Comedy* as the personified allegories of the theological virtues (*Paradise*, XX, 127).

The supernatural and spiritual role of the nymph is stressed in the Renaissance by the Italian theoretician Antonio Minturno who makes a group of nymphs the principal protagonists of his semi-pastoral work *L'amore innamorato*, published in Venice, in 1559. As they are closest to the origin of the world, notes Minturno, they are also closest to the gods.[64] For this they are the highest expression of harmony and order. *Diana's* nymphs convey harmony and order by offering hope to the grieving shepherds and shepherdess. "El remedio de vuestro mal" says the nymph Polydora, "está en manos de la discreta Felicia, a la qual dió naturaleza lo que a nosotros a negado. Y pues véis lo que os importa yr a visitarla, pídoos de parte destas nymphas... que no rehuséis nuestra compañía pues no de otra manera podéis recebir el premio de vuestro trabajo" (p. 129). In this respect the nymphs themselves take on the role of pilgrims in a journey to save souls from perdition.[65]

Evoking a distinctly Marian role, the nymph Polydora reiterates her call to the right path to the newly-found Belisa: "A lo menos podría mostrarte el camino por donde pudiesses algún poco aliviar tu pena. Y para esto te ruego que vengas en nuestra compañia, así por que no es cosa justa que tan mal gastes la vida como porque adonde te llevaremos, podrás escoger la que quisieres y no avrá persona que estorvalla pueda" (p. 160). The shepherds and shepherdesses acquiesce, and the nymphs, walking "con muy gran contentamiento... con su compañía" (p. 131), guide them toward Felicia's palace. Their guiding role is dramatized by the episode where, following the shepherd's encounter with Belisa, "un espesso bosque y tan lleno de sylvestres y espessos árboles, que a no ser de las tres nimphas guiados, no pudieran dexar de perderse en él" (p. 162).

While leading the shepherds to the palace of Lady Felicia, the nymphs continue to console their suffering companions: "No te desconsueles," says Polydora to Sireno, "que si tu dama tuviesse tan cerca el remedio de la mala vida que tiene, como tú de lo que ella te haze passar, no sería pequeño alivio para los desgustos y desabrimientos que yo sé que passa cada día" (p. 130). Seeing that the disconsolate Belisa cannot stop her bitter weeping, the nymph Dórida soothes her with these words: "Cessen, hermosa Belisa, sus lágrimas, pues vees el poco remedio dellas; mira que dos ojos no bastan a llorar tan grave mal" (p. 160). The concomitant and inspiring call to good deeds reminds us of Titian's painting, *Sacred and Profane Love*, where the two Venuses "hold sway over the two shepherds of a world within which, as Ficino puts it, love is an 'innate and uniting force that drives the higher things to care for the lower ones, the equal things to some special communion with each other, and finally induces all lower things to turn toward the better and higher ones.'"[66]

The special role of the nymphs is also underscored, symbolically, by an explicit reference to their bathing in the nude. Erwin Panofsky reminds us that nudity in the Renaissance became "invested with an almost metaphysical halo" and it came to be associated with a celestial Venus, who "leads us beyond sensory perception," in contrast to the terrestrial Venus who "rules the world of nature accessible to the eye and ear."[67] Botticelli observes this dichotomy in two famous paintings: the *Birth of Venus*, also known as *Venus Anadyomene*, where the celestial Venus, rising from the sea, is swept ashore on a shell, and the *Realm of Venus*, commonly known as *La Primavera*, where the terrestrial and carnal Venus with roses falling about her "holds gentle sway over the flowering earth."[68] In the latter stand the three graces, *Voluptas*, *Castistas*, *Pulchritudo*. That *The Twin Venuses* is held to be the more appropriate title of Titian's *Sacred and Profane Love*,[69] suggests the possible meaning inherent in the redeeming nymphs of *Diana*, carefully portrayed in their superior symbolic nudity, the only characters so represented in the novel, with the exception of Felismena, the other great inspiring force of *Diana*, who bathes with them.

As we mentioned above, the nymphs are attacked by three savages who are intent on ravishing them. The scene brings to mind Albrecht Dürer's *Rape of Proserpina*,[70] which shows the famed goddess being taken away by a wild man. Wild men are part of a long literary tradition, from classical mythology where centaurs and satyrs abound in religious writings,[71] through Chrétien de Troyes' medieval Arthurian romance, *Yvain* (vss. 288-297), to the Spanish chivalric romance *Palmerín de Inglaterra*,[72] the sentimental novel *La cárcel de amor*[73] and even in the *Quijote* (II, 20, 41). Traditionally depicted as licentious and wanton creatures in literature, folklore and medieval iconography,[74] these wild men symbolize "ugliness and bestiality"[75] in *Diana*, and form the only grotesque element in Montemayor's novel.

The three creatures who attack the peace-loving nymphs are a combination of wild men and giants, savages of "tan extraña grandeza y fealdad... que ponían espanto." In keeping with the portrayal of certain monstrous figures of Asia Minor these wild men are characterized as having "braços gruessos y vellosos... los coseletes trayan por braçales unas bocas de serpientes... y las celadas venían a hazer encima de la frente unas espantables cabeças de leones; lo demás trayan desnudo cubierto despesso y largo vello, unos bastones herrados de muy agudas púas de azero" (pp. 87-88).[76] The most repelling trait of these hideous and fierce creatures is their lasciviousness, and in this they bring to mind the raw lust of the Celtic wild man enbodied in Bremo, the wild man in *Mucedorus*, an English sixteenth-century play.[79] An object of hatred and fear in medieval folklore, wild men appear in *Diana* as the antithesis of the ideals personified by the shepherds and shepherdesses.

As diabolical figures, the savages in Montemayor's novel are like the monstrous emissaries of the devil which tear at their enemy Saint Anthony in a late fifteenth-century engraving by Martin Schongauer (Museum of Fine Arts, Boston).[78] The

Shields of *Diana's* wild men, made of tough tortoise shells, "conchas de pescado muy fuerte" (p. 88) are reminiscent of the tortoise shield engraved on a medal of Gianfrancesco Enzola of Parma (working 1456-78), depicting a horseman and two foot-soldiers wearing crestless helmets, mail and plate-armour, and using a huge live tortoise as shield.[79] In addition to the live tortoise, which may be a humorous device, the medal depicts also a spear-carrying warrior fighting a dragon, which relates, as we shall see later, not only to Felismena but also to St. George.

The prominence of the wild man in iconography, particularly as a decorative motif in fifteenth-century Gothic architecture of Spain, has been well examined by José María de Azcarate.[80] The explorations of new frontiers around the globe, as well as the vogue for chivalric romances with the legendary adventures of their heroes with giants in imaginary places, contributed notably to the diffusion of the wild-man theme in literature and pictorial representations of the sixteenth century. Consistent with the earliest iconographical representations of the savage (mid-fourteenth century) as a hairy and brutal being inclined only to the satisfaction of his animal instincts (depicted on small marble jewelry boxes and trunks, gold or silver work, manuscript borders, tapestry paintings, heraldic emblems, and later in woodcuts), the Renaissance depicts the wild man as a beast-like figure and a symbol of disordinate pleasure. One such example can be seen in the coat of arms of the Basil Wood family,[81] which shows three savages holding clubs over their right shoulders. The symbolic significance acquired by the savage in the iconographical representations of the end of the Middle Ages is illustrated in several Swiss tapestries of the time[82] and on a legend in a staircase at the University of Salamanca; as a decorative element in a door of the cathedral at Valladolid; in the house of Hernán Sánchez, in Granada; and in the Casa de las Torres, in Úbeda, just to mention a few examples.[83]

Recalling the popularity of wild men as figures in performances staged at court,[84] it is likely that the savages in *Diana*, like some other characters of the novel, are really historical figures in disguise, a clue to which may be their unconventional iron clubs tipped with sharp steel and shields made with tortoise shells. One of the best iconographical representations of wild men so depicted is found in the choir seats of St. Bavokerk (first third of the sixteenth century) in Haarlem.[85] There we see carved a savage with a mace or club in his left hand, while holding a shield with his right hand. Another wild man is depicted with hairless, naked feet, exhibiting an opening in his right leg which reveals smooth skin under the disguise. In another panel of the same choir seats there also appears a caricature of a wild man dressed in a curiously courtly attire.[86] There can be no doubt that Montemayor, who travelled to Flanders and lived there for extended periods of time, knew St. Bavokerk, and was most likely inspired to inject in his novel a representation of wild men that betrayed not only a symbolic role, but also a dramatic function in terms of their disguise.

Mythology singled out the ferocious and unpredictable wild man as "the image of winter and death and decreed his slaughter for the good of all."[87] The idea of decking the wild men with helmets that were formed in the frightening heads of lions, and corselets that were clasped with serpents' mouths may have been suggested by the masks worn by the devils in mystery plays. Representing the devil or death with heads of animals or toads is a Breton innovation,[88] and can be seen in a Corpus Christi drama performed at Aix-en-Provence in 1462.[89]

The theatrical adaptation of the wild-man theme, where men masked themselves and invited the audience to guess their identity, found a ready imitator in Montemayor whose penchant for disguise pervades the entire novel. Documented examples of wild-man plays can be traced to early thirteenth-century theatrical activity at Padua, and the vogue for such dramatic representations continued through the eighteenth century.[90]

A play known only through the Latin words *magnus ludus de homine salvatico* was the first important theatrical representation of a wild man, presented at Padua during Pentecost in 1208. Another wild-man play was held in Padua in

1224, and this time we are told that it took place *cum gigantibus*, with giants, whom we can regard at secondary figures in the play.[91] A similar theatrical performance was acted out in 1399 in Aaran, Switzerland, with the name *ludus at virum dictum wildman*.[92] In some rituals at pageants and festivals masked persons impersonated wild men so well that "they showed a marked similarity to the original wild man, creating the impression that it is not always easy or even possible to distinguish between demons of human form and their animal counterparts."[93] The frequent representation of wild-man pageants at Carnival time is itself suggestive of its potential as a dramatic tool.

A *danza de salvajes* was even used to terminate the festivities in honor of Cardinal Silíceo at his installation in Toledo, in 1545. Festivities involving wild-man impersonators were common at royal courts, as Richard Bernheimer has noted,[94] and it is possible that such rituals were part of the court entertainment that had actually been witnessed by Montemayor during his service at the courts of Charles V and Philip II. There is even a report that to amuse the French king Charles VI at a wedding feast, one of his retainers conceived a fateful pleasantry. "The young king and five other knights were to secretly dress themselves in linen coats covered with flax to resemble a hairy pelt. This masquerade pleased the king greatly. At midnight the savages appeared in a group before the wedding guests, but Charles could not resist leaving the others in order to sport with the ladies, 'as was natural to his youth.' Just then the king's brother, eager to get a better look, approached the inflammable masqueraders with a torch. In an instant, as a miniature recording the event shows, the pranksters went up in flames, four of them burning to death. Only youthful vanity and 'the providence of God' had saved the king's life."[95] The episode is captured pictorially in a work entitled *Bal d'Ardents* (British Museum; MS. Harl. 4380).

The death of the wild men by Felismena is described with vivid details: "Pues como assí viesse las tres Nimphas, y la contienda entre los dos salvages y los pastores que ya no esperavan sino la muerte, poniendo con gran presteza una aguda saeta en su arco con tan grandíssima fuerça y destreza la despidió, que al uno de los salvages se la dexó escondida en el duro pecho. De manera que la de amor quel coraçón le traspassava, perdió su fuerça y el salvage la vida, a bueltas della. Y no fué perezosa en poner otra saeta en su arco, ni menos diestra en tiralla pues fué de manera que acabó con ella las passiones enamoradas del segundo salvage, como las del primero avía acabado. Y queriendo tirar al tercero que en guarda de las tres nimphas estava no pudo tan presto hazello que él no se viniesse a juntar con ella, queriéndola herir con su pesado alfange. La hermosa pastora alçó el bastón y como el golpe descargasse sobre las barras del fino azero que tenía, el alfange fué hecho dos pedaços y la hermosa pastora le dió tan gran golpe con su bastón por encima de la cabeça que le hizo arrodillar y apuntándole con la hazerada punta a los ojos con tan gran fuerça le apretó que por medio de los sesos se lo passó a la otra parte y el feroz salvage, dando un espantable grito, cayó muerto en el suelo'' (p. 90). The death scene mars the ideal setting of peace and innocence and reminds us of the reality of the Death in Arcady theme dramatized in the earliest theatrical representations of the danse macabre, dating back to the late fourteenth century, in France and England.[96] More importantly, however, the presence of death in a campestral setting can be related to the first pictorial rendering of death in Arcady made by Giovanni Francesco Guercino in a work entitled *Et in Arcadia ego* ("Even in Arcady there I am"),[97] painted at Rome between 1621 and 1623 and now preserved in the Galleria Nazionale d'Arte Antica. The words are incised on a moldering piece of masonry on which lies a huge human skull, symbol of Death, a moral reminder of the futility of life's endeavors. A further analogue of the wild-man episode of *Diana* is found pictorially in an etching by Albrecht Dürer, dated 1503, in which there appear both a wild man embracing a woman and a skull symbol of his and every man's death. Parenthetically, a Renaissance coat of arms bearing three skulls[98] is a vivid reminder of the reference in the palace of Lady Felicia where there are "cabeças de Moros" (p. 174) depicted under the feet of a figure of the Cid engraved on a side of a bronze pillar.

The death symbolism associated with the savages in *Diana* is expanded by the reference to the setting whence they come. Whereas the waters of the *locus amoenus* are invariably described as "calmas," "puras," and "cristalinas," the river crossing the "escura y encantada selva" in which dwell the wild men is "impetuoso y turbio," a vivid symbol of the savages' deadly violence, as are the "temerosos campos" (p. 88) irrigated by their river. In addition, we will recall that the nymphs are attacked by the wild men in the field of laurels (p. 89), plants sacred to Apollo, the goddess Diana's twin brother who transformed Daphne into a laurel tree. The episode is vividly captured in the painting *Apollo and Daphne* by the early Renaissance artist Antonio Pollaiuolo (National Gallery, London). In this context, it is well to recall that in mythology, the Maenads, orgiastic priestesses of Daphne, the mountain nymph, chewed laurel leaves as an intoxicant and periodically rushed out of the woods at the full moon, assaulted unwary travellers and tore children or young animals in pieces; laurel contains cyanide of potassium.[99]

It is precisely in the laurel field that Felismena comes to the rescue of the nymphs. In another study I advance the view that Felismena, symbolically, takes on a Marian role in her defense of the nymphs and shepherds, a deed that permits the wayfarers' journey toward Felicia's palace, allegorically a *terra repromissionis sanctorum*, a holy place of reward for the toils endured by the enamoured shepherds.[100] The association of Felismena to a Marian role is not surprising if we recall the conventional prominence given by Montemayor to the Holy Virgin, as the embodiment of all Christian virtues, in his interpretation of the 86th Psalm. His exaltation of the Virgin in that work was particularly significant at a time when cults of the Blessed Mother and other saints were seen largely as obstacles to reformation efforts to put Christians on a more direct relationship with God.[101] The possibility of seeing Felismena in the role of the Blessed Mother gains strength from a lavish description of her singular beauty, for which she is deemed to be the daughter of Venus (p. 91). This having been said, the link with the Virgin is provided by no one less than the painter Albrecht Dürer: "The pagan people attributed the utmost beauty to their heathen God Abblo... thus we shall use him for Christ the Lord who is the more beautiful man, and just as they represented Venus as the most beautiful woman we shall chastely display the same feature in the image of the Holy Virgin, mother of God."[102] Not only is Felismena the most beautiful woman of the novel, she is also the most chaste, courageous and discreet. She is what Diana should be, but she is also attributed a lineage with Mars and Minerva for her valor and wisdom; in short she is the embodiment of virtue, just as the Virgin is considered a "paradigm of virtues,"[103] in Montemayor's devotional poetry. In the representative imitation of human life, not in its average but in its superior or ideal forms, *Diana*, like much of Italian Renaissance painting from Cimabue to Michelangelo, fulfills its highest function. After all, let us remember that early critics observed that poetry like painting was an imitation of nature "by which they meant human nature, and human nature not as it is, but in Aristotle's phrase, as it ought to be, 'raised,' as a modern writer has well expressed it, 'above all that is local and accidental, purged of all that is abnormal or eccentric, so as to be in the highest sense representative.'"[104]

Diana's lofty function is further conveyed as Felismena appears on the stage with a staff of wild oak, the top of which has a large steel spearhead (p. 90). In Roman antiquity the spear, not the sceptre, was the main symbol of power and authority, and in the Middle Ages it became the weapon of such courageous killers of dragons (i.e., heresies) as St. George and St. Michael. It was also, in wider terms, "the weapon of the Christian Knight the *Miles Christianus* described by Erasmus of Rotterdam and glorified in Dürer's famous engraving of 1513."[105] Before

Dürer, a fifteenth-century drawing from *Les Belles Heures* of the Duc de Berry (c. 1405), now in the Cloisters collection of the Metropolitan Museum of Art (New York), shows Saint George, patron of chivalrous knights, rescuing a beautiful princess from the clutches of young dragons and their monster mother which he kills.[106] The analogy with events in Montemayor's novel points up the fact that a significant human action, the chief business of a serious painter, in the opinion of Leon Battista Alberti,[107] is also the principal concern of Montemayor, novelist. The fact that Felismena is attributed by the nymph Dórida a lineage to Minerva for her wisdom (p. 91) is also significant in pictorial for it brings to mind Mantegna's colorful picture *Wisdom driving out the vices*. In the painting, Minerva, armed with a spear, casts out the Vices as the Virtues contemplate the battle from above, in the clouds. An inscription refers to the Mother of the Virtues who is the invisible figure of Truth. ("Et mihi virtutum matri succurite divi": "Come to my help, O Gods—to me who am the mother of virtue").[108] In both the witnessing of the battle by the Virtues and in the inscription, Mantegna's painting anticipates the scene in Montemayor's novel where Felismena kills the savages as the omniscient Lady Felicia looks on, a point revealed by Felicia who explains to Felismena upon meeting her: "Yo, sin estar informada de nadie, sé quien sóis y adonde os llevan vuestros pensamientos, con todo lo que hasta aora os a sucedido" (p. 163).

The unique place occupied by Felismena among the wayfaring shepherds and shepherdesses is dramatized by the fact that it is she who reads the moral warnings inscribed on the entrance to the palace, and it is she who call them "leyes" (p. 166). Her singular role is symbolically seen by yet another event. After receiving the gratitude of Felicia for having saved her nymphs from the wild men, only she is given a place in Felicia's own quarters so that they may converse alone (p. 171). While Selvagia and Belisa keep their rustic clothing, Felismena is singled out by being elegantly dressed by the nymphs, who adorn her with fine and highly symbolic jewels.

Following his practice of extracting a symbolic meaning from material objects in order to point a moral lesson, as seen in his early work *Exposición moral sobre el salmo LXXXVI*, Montemayor uses the jewels as carefully executed vehicles of didacticism. The intelligent examination of these precious stones made by Francisco Márquez Villanueva[109] discloses a wide range of symbolic and allegorical connotations which enrich and strengthen the instructive nature of *Diana*, while confirming the exalted role of Felismena in the novel. Crystal, with which the stems of Felismena's earrings are made, had been considered since the early Middle Ages as a symbol of the spirit.[110] With this it is quite plausible that the transparent quartz represents in *Diana* the "pureza del alma en gracia de Dios,"[111] a condition symbolized by a perfect diamond for St. Teresa of Ávila. Parenthetically, it is well to point out that Felismena's forehead is characterized as "cristalina" (p. 172), a further symbol of her freedom from fault or guilt, in contrast to Diana who is guilty of inconstancy.

The naviform earrings worn by Felismena are also highly connotative. A rare example of a gold enamelled pendant in a boat shape, probably of Venetian work, and similar to the one described by Montemayor, is in the Victoria and Albert Museum of London. Although its precise symbolism is unknown, it is known that the ship "typified the Holy Church of Christ,"[112] possibly symbolized in *Diana* by the collective body of shepherds and shepherdesses moving toward Felicia's palace under the protection of Felismena. Since Horace (*Ode* III; book 1) the ship had also been treated in conjunction with hope, and the "ship of hope" was a frequent image in secular, spiritual, and emblematic literature of the Renaissance.[113] Felismena, who heroically pursues her goal of finding her loved-one, never wavering in her mission, can truly be said to exemplify the virtue of hope. Not suprisingly, Felicia rewards the relentless Felismena with renewed and reassuring hope of fulfilling her "virtuoso fin" (p. 171) of finding Felix. The hopeful nature of Felismena is symbolized by the splendid emeralds from which her earrings are carved, whose green color is itself a symbol of hope.[114] Not only is emerald a symbol of hope, recommended for passions of the heart,[115] it is also suggestive of the resplendent just soul,[116] a quality that eminently characterizes Felismena who justly protects the nymphs and Felix from adversity.

The expressive function of Felismena's jewels is extended to the oriental pearls that garnish her headgear. In the oriental tradition the pearl awakens love in the one who bears it[117] while Christian writings beginning with St. Isidore recognize this gem as a sign of innocence and humility.[118] The union of the beautiful with the good as a conception of art was first suggested by Socrates who regarded the beautiful as coincident with the good, and both of them as resolvable into the useful. Accordingly, the philosopher minimized the importance of the immediate gratification which a beautiful object affords to perception and contemplation, and stressed instead its power in furthering the more necessary ends of life.[119] To those ends, equally significaant are the sapphires enchased in each of the two jewels that decorate the scarlet band with which Felismena is symbolically crowned. Of transparent rich blue corundum, the sapphire has been associated with the firmament and has thus come to signify "moralmente los valores de fijeza y inmutabilidad,"[120] qualities so highly representative of Felismena.

The emerging visual portrait of Felismena is part of the novelist's search to eternalize, as it were, Felismena and her virtues, in a specific moment of her life. This becomes particularly significant if we bear in mind the fact that until the Baroque the general norm was to make portraits only of nobility and others of high social rank,[121] as Felismena certainly is. Anticipating a technique frequently found in Baroque portraits, Montemayor depicts Felismena in a fantastic setting, adorned with a generous complement of objects that have a symbolic and allegorical function in relation to the character being depicted. One of the most intriguing objects to adorn Felismena is "un collar de oro fino, hecho a manera de culebra enroscada que de la boca tenía colgada una águila que entre las uñas tenía un rubí grande de infinito precio" (p. 172). The serpent in the form of a circle, *culebra enroscada*, frequently portrayed in Renaissance emblematic tradition, symbolized universality or omnipresence, and (for the reason that it offers no solution of continuity) likewise of Eternity.[122] The coiled snake is also representative of the inscrutability of the Divine Being,[123] a popular idea in Eastern architecture, and among the guild of Cathedral builders known as the Comacine Masters. At times, the coiled snake was further represented in emblematic literature as a symbol of prudence as well.[124] The symbol is worthy of Felismena whose love is unbending, and who governs and disciplines herself by the use of reason. Equally appropriate to her character is the symbol of valor and generosity associated with the eagle hanging from the serpent's mouth.[125] As for the ruby, which is encased between the claws of the eagle, it should be noted that it was not only considered the supreme gem in the Renaissance, but that it was also an object of almost sacred prestige.[126] As such it became a tremendous allegorical tool for the representation of the "símbolo perfecto del corazón enamorado,"[127] most fitting tribute to Felismena. That the vivid description of the headdress and neckware should begin and end with a ruby is indeed indicative, as Márquez Villanueva has noted, of the special significance attributed to this gem by Montemayor who professes throughout *Diana* that beauty is of spiritual-not physical origin.[128] The description of Felismena's necklace evokes the image of those emblems so popular in Renaissance and Baroque Europe whose history has been perceptively traced by Mario Praz[129] and Karl Ludwig Selig,[130] among others. Although, as Francisco Márquez Villanueva has noted, no such precious object has been preserved from the sixteenth century, it does appear in a celebrated portrait of Simonetta Vespucci done by Piero di Cosimo.[131] The portrait found in the Musee Condé de Chantilly is said to represent Simonetta as Prosperina,[132] daughter of Ceres, goddess of grain and harvest. Parenthetically, it is worth noting that a character named Prosperina, a pleading figure, appears in the song of Orpheus in Poliziano's pastoral opera *Orfeo* (verses 286-301), written in 1480. In *Diana*, Orpheus will dedicate his song first to Felismena, and then to the other guests at Felicia's palace. In the portrait of Simonetta Vespucci, a woman beloved of princes and painters, and often referred to as "The Perfect Beauty," the snake is intended to symbolize her death from consumption (tuberculosis) and perhaps also to link her with the great beauty of antiquity, Cleopatra.[133]

A representation of a figure similar to that found on Felismena's necklace appears also in a medal attributed to Niccoló Fiorentino (1430-1514) and in two emblems of Joachim Camerarius and George Wither, both posterior to the publication of *Diana*.[134] Discussing the influence of Wither's emblems on the work of Crashaw, the critic Marc F. Bertonasco affirms: "George Wither provides us with an interesting example of a reproduction of one of Camerarius' plates: an eaglet is perched on a winged ball, which in turn rests on an altar. On each side serpents unsuccessfully attack the bird. Virtue aspires to sublime heights and is indifferent both to earthly blessings, which it sees as ephemeral and fickle and to the attacks of worldlings."[135] The eagle, then, represents as Frederick A. de Armas has noted, the flight toward perfection and virtue,[136] qualities so eminently displayed by Felismena.

The allegorical moralizing that Montemayor conveys in his highly symbolic treatment of Felismena's jewelry is not suprising in a man purported to have been the son of a silversmith and said to have written a book on blazons,[137] an enigmatic art-form that represents heraldic and armorial bearings. The scrupulous attention to detail that characterizes the description of Felismena's attire and jewels relates to "the immense care and learning which was spent on the 'correct' equipment of figures not only in paintings but also in masques and pageantries where nobody but the organizers themselves could ever hope to understand all the learned allusions lavished on the costumes of figures which would only appear for a fleeting moment. Perhaps the idea was under the threshold of consciousness that by being in the 'right' attire these figures became genuine 'masks' in the primitive sense, which turn their bearers into the supernatural beings they represent. Justice welcoming the King at the city gate during a 'Glorious Entry' was perhaps conceived as more than just a pretty girl wearing a strange costume. In and through her, Justice herself had come down to earth to greet the ruler and to act as a spell and an augury.'' [138] Writing about the Latin pastoral, Bruno Snell observes that the heritage of the Greeks is turned, in Virgil's *Eclogues*, into "allegory, and literature is transformed into a kingdom of symbols."[139] That strain of allegory and symbolism is amplified in *Diana* as the shepherds continue their pilgrimage to the palace of the wise Felicia.

On the way to the palace, Felismena gives an account of her life, a story laden with symbolism. Literarily and artistically important in that story is the report that her parents Delia and Andronio once spent the greater part of a night arguing the question whether the archtype of the shepherd Paris (son of Priam, King of Troy) gave the apple to the right goddess or not, and whether the inscription on it referred to physical or spiritual beauty (pp. 97-98). According to mythology, Paris, with the alternatives clearly before him, chooses Venus. Of the three ideals represented by the goddesses Venus, Juno, and Pallas Athena, or Minerva, only beauty has any significant power in myth and pastoral life, at least until *Diana* as we shall soon see. Significantly, too, Paris is the judge precisely because the conditions of the pastoral life provide the greatest independence, the greatest security. The shepherd is not motivated by ambition or greed. Free from these two common human passions, he pursues, instead, beauty, and loves the beholder of it.[140]

Historically, the Paris story was a common subject of the pageants—for Queen Margaret at Edinburgh in 1503, for the coronation of Anne Boleyn in 1533, and at a marriage masque in 1566.[141] The tale of Paris enjoyed such vogue in Renaissance art that a sixteenth-century Italian treatise on painting in making clear the artist's obligations of representing "not only the proper and natural emotions but also the diversities of affections and passions in one body," uses the temptation of Paris as an example.142 The story appeared in emblem-books, among them Whitney's *Choice of Emblems* (1586, p. 83); it is engraved in a medal by an unknown sixteenth-century artist,143 and is the subject by an important painting by Bertoia (School of Parma), a contemporary of Montemayor. The painting is particularly relevant to *Diana* for its synthesises visually several of the motifs found in the novel: nocturnal Diana (goddess Diana with crescent moon in the painting), satyr with nymph, shepherds with sheep, hills and mountains, and a temple with obelisks and tombs, such as we have in Felicia's palace (National Gallery of Art, Washington, D,C.). The Paris myth is also treated after Montemayor in two famous paintings by Rubens,144 one showing Paris with a cayado, "sheep hook," Hermes (called Mercury by the Romans) with wings on his hat and holding the apple (Prado, Madrid), the other depicting Paris with the the golden apple, Hermes standing behind him and both watching attentively the three goddesses, Juno (with the peacock), Venus (in the middle), and Minerva, with a vision of Eris, goddess of discord above, overlooking the Judgment (London, National Gallery).

In Renaissance art and literature, the classical tale can either adorn a tale or convey a moral lesson. The moral direction stems from the interpretation of the myth as "a trial of pleasure against virtue"145 given by Athanaeus and Fulgentius, and underscored in the Renaissance by Ficino who completed and refined the allegorical meaning suggested by Fulgentius:146 the three rival goddesses, Juno, Pallas or Minerva, and Venus represent, respectively, the life of action, the life of contemplation, and the life of pleasure. Paris's choice of Venus as the most beautiful of the deities became a cause of lively debate among sixteenth-century humanists as well as literary characters. Among the latter are Delia and Andronio, parents of Felismena in Montemayor's *Diana*. In Book II Delia contends that it should be given "a la más hermosa"of the goddesses, this beauty, "no se entendía corporal, sino del ánima" (p. 98). This interpretation, which finds ready acceptance among the composers of emblems and didactic lyrics of the Renaissance,[147] adds yet another facet to the over-all moral current of *Diana*.

In yet another parallel with the visual arts, the conjured image of Arsenio holding a "ballesta" (p. 158) is akin to that of Death in a scene of the Dance of Death by the sixteenth-century Swiss artist Nicolas Manuel Deutsch.[148] Widely used since the Han dynasty of China, the cross-bow was a leading instrument of war in the Middle Ages. By then, the danger of the cross-bow had spread so alarmingly through Europe that Pope Innocent II decreed the weapon "too barbarous" for one Christian to use against another.[149] The instrument is shown in an illustration *Hunter shooting an arbalest*, in *Les Chroniques d'Angleterre*,[150] and its barbarity is dramatized by Antonio and Piero del Pollaiuolo in their artistic representation, the *Martyrdom of St. Sebastian*, in which two crossbowmen, fore and aft, are setting their bows, while another shoots a bolt (or quarrel) into the saint's back.[151] In the Renaissance, when the cross-bow was quickly being replaced by other martial devices, it continued to remain a frightful symbol of death, a symbol that Montemayor skilfully employs in the concocted death scene of Arsenio's son, Arsileo.

The scene in which Arsenio presumably kills his son takes place as Arsileo climbs into a mulberry tree, next to the house of his beloved Belisa. We will recall that in the story of Pyramus and Thisbe (Ovid's *Metamorphoses*, IV: 55: 166), Pyramus kills himself when he sees Thisbe's shawl covered with blood (cow's blood as it turns out, mauled by a lion), and his blood turns red the previously white mulberry. The mythological tale is captured pictorially by Nicolas Manuel Deutsch, showing Thisbe taking her own life with a sword, following Pyramus' death (Kunstmuseum, Basel).

Incidentally, Arsenio, a wealthy landlord, who appears in *Diana* in the shadow of his son Arsileo, the real object of Belisa's love, displays several traits common to Pantalone, that memorable character in the *Commedia dell'arte* shown in an illustration of about 1550 accompanying a French rendition of a *Commedia dell'arte* play.[152] The other two figures depicted with *Pantalone*, the comical Harlequin and the rascal Corneto, bring to mind two more characters of *Diana*, respectively, Montano who sings "Amor loco ¡ay amor loco! / yo por vos y vos por otro" (p. 57), and the servant of shameless resourcefulness, Fabio, who connives with Felismena to make her Don Felix's page.

Literature and art come together again in the novel's description of a sculpture depicting the history of Lucretia, the Roman heroine who killed herself after having been violated by Sextus Tarquinius. The sculpture, we are told, is so vividly carved that it approaches photographic realism: "tan al natural que verdaderamente parecía que Lucrecia acabava allí de darse muerte" (p. 177). Titian records the violent seduction in one of his early paintings, while another sixteenth-century artist, Jan Gossaert, focuses on the suicide of the heroine (*Lucretia*, 1532), giving us a visually expressive image as in the statue of Lucretia in Felicia's palace.

Diana's relationship to the visual arts is further strengthened by the novel's treatment of another vivid reminder of death, the tombs. Felicia's garden, we will recall, houses countless graves of nymphs and ladies "las quales avían, con gran limpieza, conservado la castidad devida a la castíssima Diosa [Diana]" (p. 191). For their steadfastness, these women have acquired glory, and are immortalized in an allegorical conception of what is, after all, a temple of fame, itself a model to its wayfaring visitors.[155] In the middle of the garden, the author tells us, "estava una piedra negra, sobre quatro pilares de metal, y en medio della un sepulcro de jaspe que quatro nimphas de alabastro en las manos sostenían; en torno dél, estavan muchos blandones y candeleros de fina plata, muy bien labrados, y en ellos hachas blancas ardiendo; en torno de la capilla, avía algunos bultos de cavalleros, y damas, unos de metal, otros de alabastro, otros de mármol jaspeado, y de otras diferentes materias" (p. 191).

The sepulchre amidst a sylvan setting finds an artistic parallel in Nicolas Poussin's memorable painting *Et in Arcadia Ego* where shepherds point to these words carved on a tomb under the watchful eyes of a sybil. The most famous tomb in *Diana* is that of Lady Catalina of Aragon y Sarmiento, a woman praised in history and in literature for her outstanding faith and goodness. The candlesticks with burning tapers symbolize these virtues. "It behoveth man," says a twelfth-century writer, "to have a candlestick that he may shine with good works,"[154] and there is a 1488 inscription on a candlestick which "by its good example inflameth others."[155] A century later Shakespeare exclaims "How far that little candle throws his beams! So shines a good deed in a naughty world."[156] Lady Catalina's tomb provides the shepherds and shepherdesses with a model in their pilgrimage toward "grace." The tomb also points up the fact that in its entirety Felicia's palace guards the highest virtues of true lovers (constancy and chastity), which are contrasted to the condition of change and lascivious love, exemplified by the shepherdess Diana and the wild men, respectively.[157] In defense of the virtue of the visual image, Ficino expressed the view that the right image engraved on the right stone may have a potent effect on health.[158] The efficiency of the combined image and stone touches spiritual health as well, for the visual image is morally instructive: "knowledge through symbols is higher knowledge."[159] Indeed the sculptured figures adorning the tomb of Lady Catalina touched the heart of the beautiful Felismena and all who stood looking at the tomb (pp. 191-192). The symbolism of Lady Catalina's tomb is enhanced by a figure holding a metal tablet at the base of the tomb wherein is inscribed the following epitaph:

>Aquí reposa doña Catalina
>de Aragón y Sarmiento, cuya fama
>al alto cielo llega y se avezina
>y desde el Bórea al Austro se derrama;
>matéla, siendo muerte tan aína
>por muchos que ella a muerto, siendo dama;

acá está el cuerpo; el alma, allá en el cielo,
que no la mereció gozar el suelo (p. 192).

The emblem, the device, not only instructs us but, as E.H. Grombrich points out, it "affects us." Arguments may convince, he goes on to say, but, "images have a more direct impact on our mind. He who *sees* the truth can no longer err. He who is granted vision of the supra-natural ideas becomes attuned to them."[160] That message is captured by the tomb and epitaph of Doña Mencía de Mendoza, daughter of the great Castilian poet, the Marqués de Santillana. The tomb, designed by Alonso Berrugulte (c. 1486-1561), was made with the Italian marble and is characterized by beautiful carvings, a wealth of detail and a peaceful and robust figure of the famed Castilian lady in a recumbent effigy (Chapel of the Constable, Burgos Cathedral).[161]

Through the inscription and the representation of tombs of nymphs and noble ladies *Diana* presents the underlying thought that "man in his fallen state is a prey to death, but man redeemed inherits eternal life."[162] The inevitability of death, suggested in *Diana*, is not a Christian theme, "unless it is completed by some reference to the resurrection or the redemption of man."[163] Montemayor's novel eminently fulfills this requirement by "resurrecting" its characters from their *desengaño*, from their misdirected passions to a new rational life through the allegorically sacramental intervention of Lady Felicia.

The redeemimg quality of death is exemplified pictorially in the vast anonymous fresco of the Last Judgment found in the Basilique Ste. Cecile, at Albi[164] (late fifteenth—early sixteenth centuries). The fresco is important for it avoids linking the end of physical being with physical decay, stressing instead, as in Montemayor's novel, the lofty aspects of death, a fact which explains the virtual absence of macabre references to death in *Diana*.

The moral dimension of *Diana* in its relationship to the visual arts is expanded by the identification of Felicia's palace with the

Temple of Diana, highly symbolic in terms of the shepherds' pilgrimage and their ultimate marriages. Montemayor's readers knew very well what the Temple of Diana meant, says T. Anthony Perry, "or at least they knew that it signified 'chastity,' and they probably realized, too, that the veil of mystery would be lifted to the degree that they perceived the meaning in their lives as well as their critical minds."[165] To the perceptive reader of the time the temple in Montemayor's novel must have been analogous to that of the so-called goddess Diana Tifalina, whose temple on Mt. Tifalus was consecrated to this goddess as protectress of conjugal fidelity.[166] Traditionally associated with water, trees, wild vegetation and woodland-life, Diana Tifalina was also identified with the moon. In Montemayor's novel, Diana is identified with the lunar deity in Orpheus' song (p. 184), in a reference to Arsileo's journey to the temple to meet Belisa (p. 246), and in the epitaph of a nymph (p. 192). Parenthetically, the lunar goddess was worshipped among the Greeks as Artemis, the pure and spotless one. It is interesting to note that in emblematic representations of the Renaissance Diana is often depicted with a crescent moon on her head, symbol of heaven in early Christian symbolism, and an illustration of the mystic lady so depicted is found in two sixteenth-century watermarks reproduced in Harold Bayley's *A New Light on the Renaissance*.[167]

Furthermore, an unidentified member of the School of Fountainbleau depicted Diana of Poitiers as Diana the Huntress crowned with a crescent moon (Louvre, 16th century). In his *Diana surprised by Actaeon* Titian, too, shows Diana with the crescent moon in her headdress while showing one of the nymphs with a mirror, bringing back the image, noted earlier, of the shepherdess Diana combing her hair in front of a mirror being held by Sireno. In Montemayor's novel, an important reference is made to nocturnal Diana, who illuminates the green valleys for the shepherds of the novel while the nymphs and the shepherdesses rejoice in a religious ceremony, complete with prayers and offerings, in the sacred Temple of Minerva (pp. 41-42). A painting of this temple done by the eighteenth-century artist R. Wilson (London, Brinsley Ford Collection) is similar in shape to the temple in Bertoia's previously-cited work *The Judgment of Paris*, and its smallness evokes the intimate gathering of the shepherds, in *Diana's* Temple of Minerva. The splendorous light cast by the moon goddess may well be a prelude to the spiritual enlightenment that the characters will experience in *Diana's* own temple.

Doubtless *Diana* is a *roman á clef*. The author defines it as such in the Argument, Lope de Vega later confirms it, and it appears that King Philip III, Queen Margarita and her courtiers interpreted the novel as a work hiding a meaning.[168] Similarly, as Maxime Chevalier observes, Parisian publishers of the sixteenth and seventeenth centuries accounced in the titles, annotations, and advertisements of their editions of *Diana* the novel's varied hidden meanings.[169] This is not surprising, for "The form and content of the novel, even the novel of fantasy," as notes Michael Zeraffa, "describe more closely from social phenomena than do those of other arts, except perhaps cinema; novels often seem bound up with particular moments in the history of society."[170] Appropriately, Francisco López Estrada recommends that *Diana* not be elevated above the existence of the author, but rather be placed within the very course of his life.[171]

Montemayor spent considerable time in the Netherlands and his presence there is picked up by Jean Subirats whose perceptive study charts new inroads into the novel's frame of disguise.[172] According to Subirats, the central episodes of *Diana* are to be related to festivals at the Château Ténébreux at Binche (August 22-31, 1549), by order of the regent Mary of Hungary in honor of then Prince Philip, feasts at which were present the elite of the Spanish nobility. Specifically, these feasts are identified, appearing under pastoral disguise, in Books IV and V of *Diana*: the powerful Felicia is Mary of Hungary, and the nymphs are ladies of the Spanish court who have disguised themselves as nymphs during the festivities. The disposition of Felicia's palace is typical of a Renaissance château, similar to the one at Binche,[173] and Subirats has also pointed out parallels between the interior of Felicia's palace, with its abundance of "marble," "jasper," "alabaster," and its "golden pillars" and "double leafed windows," with the interior of the palace at Binche,[174] highly renowned for its magnificence. In his representation of Felica's palace, and the events that take place in it, it is indeed possible that Montemayor wished to immortalize the famous fêtes of Binche, to give the feasts a halo of legend.[175]

Subirats' connection is made even more plausible by the documented report of another episode linking *Diana* to the feasts at Binche. Vicente Alvarez reports that a stunning event at these feasts was a dramatic performance of actors dressed as "wild men" attempting to kidnap some beautiful women,[176] dramatic representations "symbolizing a force hostile to society,"[177] like similar events in Book II of *Diana*. Those representations are recorded pictorially in several works of the time including one entitled "Divertissement dans la grande salle du palais de Binche, 1549. Combat des chevaliers et des sauvages. Enlèvement des dames."[178] A detail of that drawing points out clearly Mary of Hungary, Charles V, Eleanor of Austria, and Prince Philip,[179] sitting in the foreground, as the performers act out their parts as wild men and ladies who are about to ravished by them. Other drawings of events at Binche collected by Daniel Devoto show both the exterior of the Château Ténébreaux, with visible similarities to the "sumptuous"palace of lady Lady Felicia (e.g. turrets, some double arched windows), and certain welcoming ceremonies outside the palace.[180]

Mesmerized by their new surroundings, the shepherds approach a silver fountain in the middle of the inner court next to which sits Orpheus, whose music, in legend, enchanted all the wild beasts, trees, and rocks on Olympus, and made cruel beasts mild and humble.[181] Montemayor must have been intrigued by the figure of Orpheus even before the writing of *Diana* since in one of his religious poems he pays tribute to the singer Francisco de Gracia by calling him an "Orfeo Cristiano" (*Segundo*

Cancionero, 1558, ff. 203r-204v).[182] The introduction of Orpheus into the pages of *Diana* evokes a variety of emotional situations associated with the myth of Orpheus and Eurydice, including love, death, suspense, and rescue from danger. If we remember that Orpheus was the poetic child of Apollo, the presence of the mythical singer in Felicia's palace is exquisitely justified. This will become clear in the pages ahead where we shall treat the Felicia-Apollo-Christ relationship. Orpheus, like the shepherds gathered in Felicia's palace for whom he performs, was also overcome by love and anxiety, but the use that Montemayor makes of him in *Diana* transcends this simple comparison. He is actually "resurrected" to inspire the shepherds to do good deeds, and in thus moving them away from their spiritual demise he serves out, symbolically at least, his traditional characterization as a psychopomp,[183] a guide of the souls after death.

As the legendary singer is approached by the nymphs, he takes up his harp and, turning to Felismena, begins to sing. Significantly, Orpheus avoids the use of a wind instrument, traditionally seen as appealing to the baser parts of the soul (St. Clement, *Paedogogus*, II, iv), and plays instead the harp, the "noble" instrument by which David, God's helper, gave aid and comfort to Saul, thereby softening his evil spirit.[184] To be noted, particularly in terms of Diana's pilgrimage, is that the lyre, and its offshoot, the harp, connected Orpheus with a body of Neoplatonic ideas about the harmony of the universe and the return of the soul to its celestial home.[185] We remember, too, that in mythology Orpheus played an important part in the expedition of the Argonauts (band of heroes sailing with Jason in quest of the Golden Fleece), and that with his lyre he enabled them to resist the lure of the Sirens. The author of *Diana* is surely aware of this myth as he introduces Orpheus' music and song to help the group of wayfaring shepherds check their temptations.

The position of the Song of Orpheus right between the narratives of the shepherds' infirmity of passion and the cure of that passion by Felicia is indeed significant in terms of the traditional association of the myth of Orpheus with the theme of controlling disordinate desires, as represented on a Greek amphora at Karlsruhe showing the Underworld in the foreground and Orpheus subjugating Cerberus, the triple-headed Hound of Hell.[186] Representing Orpheus in hell is a bronze plaque by Peter Vischer (the Elder? 1460?-1429) showing the mythical figure with a lira da braccio.[187] Three other visual examples of Orpheus with the lyre are provided by a mosaic in the Sparta Museum, in which Orpheus is surrounded by a variety of animals, a sculptured relief in the National Museum of Naples, depicting Orpheus with Eurydice and Hermes, and a carving found in the Byzantine Museum of Athens.[188]

The harp, instrument played by Orpheus in Montemayor's novel, is an ancient instrument which can be traced to Egyptian hieroglyphics.[189] It is one of seven instruments associated with Orpheus.[190] The substitution of the harp for the lyre, the most widely cited Orphic instrument, is first mentioned in Spain by Iñigo López de Mendoza, the Marquis of Santillana, in his *Deçir que fizo el Marqués de Santillana en loor de la reina de Castilla*: "Caliope se levante / E con la harpa d'Orpheo / Las vuestras virtudes cante..."[191] Juan de Mena, a contemporary of Santillana, provides another panegyric of the Orphic harp in his *Laberinto de Fortuna* "Mostróse la harpa que Orfeo tañía / quando al infierno lo traxo el amor,"[192] while Alonso Proaza, famed corrector of *La Celestina*, picks up this characterization of the mythic singer "La harpa de Orpheo e dulce armonía / Forçaua las piedras a venir a su son / Abríe los palacios del triste Plutón..."[193]

A rare visual representation of Orpheus playing the harp is a painting executed in Rouen, in 1551, titled *Orphée et les Muses*, to commemorate the entrance of Henry II in that city the year before. In that painting Orpheus is shown playing an "Irish harp" to which we referred above. Interesting in terms of *Diana* is the arch of heaven over Orpheus' head centered by a crescent moon,[194] associated, as we noted earlier, with the goddess Diana, in whose temple Montemayor's Orpheus performs. The same painting also depicts five muses playing bowed instruments, and, on the right, Hercules killing the hydra.[195]

In another painting of the early sixteenth century carried out in observance of the entrance of Charles V in Bruges, in 1515, Orpheus is shown playing a bowed instrument in an orchard in the presence of two wild men with clubs, another reminder of *Diana's* link with the visual arts.[196] That link is reaffirmed as the author informs the reader that the shepherds and shepherdesses listen to the celebrated Orpheus singing the way he sang "al tiempo que en la tierra de los Ciconios cantava, quando Cipariso fué convertido en ciprés y Atis, en pino" (p. 179). Cyparissus, we will recall, was a Greek youth loved by Apollo who accidentally killed one of Apollo's favorite stags. That act made Cyparissus so disconsolate that he asked Apollo to turn him into a cypress tree, which has since remained a tree of mourning. Attis, on the other hand, was a devotee of the earth goddess Cybele, who maimed himself under a pine tree, died, his spirit entered the tree, and from his blood violets began to grow. The sacred pine tree (decked with votive objects and pine cones representing new life) and a sacrificial bull and ram is depicted in a relief from an altar to Cybele, shown in Joseph L. Henderson and Maud Oakes, *The Wisdom of the Serpent: The Myth of Death, Rebirth and Resurrection* (New York: Braziller, 1963), p. 118. At the time of Attis and Cyparrisus, Orpheus, we are told, stupefied Thracian warriors with his music, a scene conveyed on a Greek vase painted about 450 B.C.,[197] and he played his golden tones in such a way as to tame the animals of the wild, a scene recreated in a drawing by Cima da Corregliano (c. 1459—c. 1517) found in the Uffizi Gallery of Florence.

The miraculous effect ascribed to music by the ancient Greeks, "the legends of Amphion and Orpheus, the stories of Pythagoras, Plato's beliefs in the... ennobling powers of music, all were constantly in the minds of the Rennaissance musicians."[198] The effects of song and music on the spirit of man were emphasized in the Renaissance, under the influence of the Neoplatonism of Marsilio Ficino, and by such respected musicologists as Anríquez de Valderrábano in the Prologue to his *Silva de sirenas* (Valladolid, 1547) and Juan Bermudo in his *Declaración de instrumentos* (Osuna, 1549-1555). As Castiglione reminds us, music has the power to "induce a good new habit of mind and an inclination to virtue, rendering the soul more capable of happiness, just as corporal exercise makes the body more robust."[199] The best synthesis of the sixteenth-century Neoplatonists' views on music, as it relates to the spiritual wellbeing of man, is given by a leading authority of the time, Anríquez de Valderrábano:

> Sócrates (que fue tenido entre los philosóphos de su tiempo como verdadero oráculo) dezía que quando se iuntauan en el ánimo todos los desseos, affectos y movimientos della, y obedecían a la razón, se hazía de todo, como de bozes acordes, una armonía tan excelente y suaue, que despertaua al hombre y le hazía venir en consideración del mouimiento y consonancia de los cielos; y a ésta llamaua él verdadera música, y no sin causa, ca el entendimiento del hombre música es de gran perfectión, que con él se acuerdan las potencias sensitivas e intellectiuas, de do nace la consonancia de la razón, del conoscer, del sentir, del entender, y del juzgar lo bueno para huir lo malo. De que el diuino Platón dezía que la música principalmente, fue dada para templar y moderar los affectos y passiones del alma. Fue tan estimada, que para encarecer la philosophía el mismo Platón y antes del los Pithagóricos la llamaron música por serle semejante en los effectos.[200]

In one Orphic legend, we will recall, the Thracian singer used music to placate the suffering of Eurydice and to bring her back to life, a scene rendered pictorially in the *Death and Restoration of Eurydice*, from the *Ovide Moralisé* (Paris, 1493, 131r).

Orpheus' song, true to legend, has such a mesmerizing effect on the pilgrim shepherds "que a nadie se le acordava de cosa que por él uviesse passado" (p. 179), and the author later emphasizes that "assí los tenía suspensos, como si por ninguno dellos uviera passado más de lo que presente tenían" (p. 191). In Spanish music of the sixteenth century with texts in the vernacular, writes Don Randel, "nothing is reserved as belonging strictly in the province of only the secular or only the sacred,"201 an observation that further strengthens the spirituality-edifying component of Orpheus' music. The spiritual dimension of Orpheus' music is captured visually in an eight-century psalter with a sketch *David and Melodia* showing Orpheus in the guise of David playing the lyre (dated between the eighth and the eleventh centuries). In that painting a richly clad David is surrounded by animals—sheep, goats and a dog—and by three allegorical figures, along with a nymph, and Melodia, the mountain goddess wearing a laurel fillet on her brow, and reclining in the traditional attitude of the Nile god.202 Orpheus is again identified with David, in a work by Bartholomeo Passerotti (*King David*, Galleria Spada, Rome), shown with a lira da braccio, which in the miniatures and woodcuts of the late quattrocento begins to replace the harp of King David.203 Placing Orpheus in a Christian context, which is precisely the case in Montemayor's novel, goes back to the early Middle Ages, as recorded pictorially in a series of revealing drawings, reliefs, and frescoes, among them one, *Orpheus figure from the Roman catacombs*, of the third or fourth centures A.D., showing a crucified man. Above the cross are a crescent moon, and seven stars, and across and below it is the legend OPTEOC BAKKIKÓC. "Just as Christ is to be seen in Christian monuments with the attributes of Orpheus, so here, by a tribute from the other side, Orpheus is represented in the attitude of Christ."204 Furthermore, an Orpheus fresco (Cemetery of the Two Laurels, Rome, c. fourth century), shows Orpheus sitting in the frontal or Imperial pose, typical of the art of the fourth and later centuries, holding the plectrum in his right hand and the lyre in his left. A dove and an eagle perched on each side of Orpheus in trees together with the central figure serve as an emblem for the Christian soul in this life and the next, giving us what is in effect another portrait of Orpheus—Christus.205

The fusion of Pagan-Christian mysteries is also revealed in a sarcophagus relief from Porto-Torres, Sardinia, which shows Christ in the pose of Mithras Tauroctonus, but wearing the

Phrygian costume of Orpheus.[206] A mosaic of Orpheus from Jerusalem (sixth century) continues to depict Christ in the aspect of Orpheus (mosaic presently in the Archaeological Museum of Istanbul). Orpheus—Christus sits in the frontal pose of Byzantine art, surrounded by birds and other animals. Below Orpheus' lyre stands Pan holding his syrinx (panpipe) and pointing to a centaur resting below the eagle at Orpheus' right.[207]

To Neoplatonists "the myths were not only a mine of edifying metaphors. They were in fact yet another form of revelation. In accepting this belief the Neo-Platonists had no intention of minimizing the value of the Bible as the chief instrument of Divine revelation. On the contrary, they were convinced that the pagan lore rightly understood could only point towards the same truth which God had made manifest through the Scripture."[208] That pagan traditions were often not compatible with Christianity is seen in Petrarch's reaction to Cicero's *De natura deorum* in which the Italian humanist believed to have heard not the voice of a pagan philosopher but of an apostle.[209] Similarly, Pico della Mirandola's *Teologia Platonica*, a work dealing with classical material, is also profoundly Christian. The great enthusiasm shown by Ficino and other Neoplatonists of his school for Horapollo Niliacus' *Hieroglyphica*, a work that claims to decipher the sacred symbols used in ancient Egypt, is another example of the way great minds of the Renaissance thrived on searching for spiritual meanings in mythical episodes of antiquity.[210] Looking at the entire universe as a great myth "endowed with spiritual meaning," Neoplatonists of Roman antiquity and of the Renaissance defended those mythological legends which Cicero and Seneca scorned as "absurdities" and gave them pious and philosophical explanations.[211]

This task was particularly easy in treating Orpheus, who was after all considered not only the first singer of antiquity and extraordinary poet, but was also seen as the principal theologian of Greece who instituted the mysteries to pacify the gods and save men.212 He was thought to have established the Orphic sect, and his disciples composed books to propagate his ideas, his theogony, purifying formulas and sacred hymns, all of which were attributed by his followers to Orpheus himself.213 The consideration of Orpheus as theologian persisted well into the seventeenth century in Spain with Fray Baltasar de Vitoria's *Primera parte del teatro de los dioses de la gentilidad*.214

It is in the sixteenth century, however, that the Christianization of Orpheus is vigorously promoted, and he is depicted as "God's minister of earth," and compared to the saints, specifically to St. John the Baptist.215 St. John, we remember, preached repentance, "for the kingdom of heaven is at hand" (Mt. 3:2), and for this he was called upon to "Prepare the way of the Lord, make his paths straight" (Mt. 3:3). It is in this context that Orpheus, in Montemayor's novel, attains his highest significance, by serving as an inspirational force to the weary pilgrims, and as the messenger and "angel" of Felicia that paves the way for the imminent and miraculous intervention.

After listening to Orpheus' music and song, the shepherds and shepherdesses become engaged in a lengthy conversation about the nature of love with Lady Felicia. The mother of love is Reason, says Felicia, but the child is unruly, and easy prey to passion, and, because of this, most characters of *Diana* "se vienen a desamar a sí mismos, que es contra razón y derecho de naturaleza" (p. 196). The ensuing debate on reason versus passion brings to mind the well-known painting by Baccio Bandinelli called *Combat of Ratio and Libido* in which Apollo and the goddess Diana (along with Mercury, Saturn, Hercules and Jupiter in their train) are the champions of virtue, while Venus (Diana in Montemayor's novel), together with Cupid and Vulcan, represent the side of Passion. Significantly, in the sky above the pictorial battle, Reason herself takes part in the conflict by shedding light on her fellow combatants, very much the way Felicia illuminates the nymphs that serve her in the cause of restoring the shepherds' proper exercise of the mind.216

In checking the rustics' amorous passion and in

circumventing what Fortune had stored for the shepherds and shepherdesses, Felicia can also be related to the figure of Virtus, in a coin representation by Niccolò Fiorentino (1430-1514) showing Virtue subduing Love and Fortune, referred to in *Diana* as the "autores de trabajo y sinrazones" (p. 167). In this emblem, called *Virtuti Omnia Parent*, Virtus, as young man, with long hair, wearing cuirass, greaves and boots, stands in the front and with his right hand he holds by the hair Love, winged, nude, blindfolded, his hands tied behind his back, quiver slung at his side, broken bow on the ground; with his left hand, Virtus holds by the hair Fortune, nude.[217] In addition to noting Felicia's role in controlling Love and Fortune, it is also well to point out that two of the virtuous women cited by Orpheus in Montemayor's novel, doña Mencía and doña Leonor Manuel are praised because one is a lady to whom "se rinde amor y se somete" (p. 190) and the other for being "la que está domando a la fortuna / y a su pesar la tiene allí rendida" (p. 182).

Before they journey to Felicia's palace the lovers are skeptical about the possibility of any remedy for their suffering. Sireno is convinced that every available option has already been exhausted (p. 130), and Belisa doubts that even time will cure her ills (p. 159). Like wayfarers in exile, estranged from God, the characters of *Diana* ultimately find a solution for their grief in the true home of love, the spiritual abode that is Felicia's palace. There lies the shepherds' only remedy: the miraculous intervention of Lady Felicia and what can rightly be called her "sacramental" water. "Olvidado pastor" says Felicia to Sireno, "si en tus males uviera otro remedio sino éste, yo te le buscara con toda la diligencia" (p. 223). "Confiad en Dios" says the sage lady to Felismena, "que vuestro desseo avrá buen fin, porque si yo de otra manera lo entendiera, bien podéis creer que no me faltarán otros remedios para hazeros mudar el pensamiento, como a algunas personas lo he hecho" (p. 223).

Unwilling to sustain the artificial passion tormenting his characters, the author resorts to a symbolic action with which he transforms the literary enigma of amorous impossibility into human love fulfilled. It is true, as Gustavo Correa has observed, that the transformation is brought on by the actions of super-human entities (nymphs, the wise Felicia, and the goddess Diana) but the solution to misguided passion comes only "al final de una vía purificatoria en el ejercicio del amor humano, el cual se ha tornado en arduo camino de renunciamiento y heroísmo".[218] The process of spiritual purification continues in Felicia's palace, seen as a "mirror of the noble soul,"[219] where virtue is repeatedly extolled. The sage lady, the mythical Orpheus, and the sacred cemetery of nymphs and noble ladies in Book IV inspire virtuous sentiments in the shepherds and shepherdesses and, by extension, graces them with a degree of wisdom, prerequisite to salvation. In this respect, the novel becomes a guide and teacher of men, complementing the instructive intent of the visual arts whose beneficial effects had been assiduously catalogued by Leon Battista Alberti.

Redemption for the characters of *Diana* begins when Sireno, from a vessel of fine crystal with a golden base, is given a magic potion which entirely removes his affection for Diana. Another "cruet," similarly made, is divided between Sylvano and Selvagia who have been grieving, respectively, for Diana and Alanio. On drinking the potions, these individuals fall insensible to the ground. A few moments afterwards, Felicia awakens Sireno by touching him upon the head with a book which she has taken out of her sleeve (p. 225). She then similarly awakens Sylvano who, on getting to his feet, cries out: "¡O Selvagia, quán gran locura a sido aver empleado en otra parte el pensamiento, después que mis ojos te vieron!"(p. 226). Without avail he tries to awaken Selvagia. Felicia directs him to an adjoining room, and then awakens Selvagia as she did the other two. Selvagia's first words are: "Señora, ¿qué es del mi Sylvano? ¿No estava él junto conmigo? ¡Ay, Dios! ¿quien me lo llevó de aquí? ¡Si bolverá! (p. 227). Three significant points are to be noted in this account: first, that the change is brought about by a draught of magic liquid which induces sleep; second, that the persons are awakened, not naturally, but by the touch of a book; third, that the altered affection is predetermined by Felicia, not dependent upon the first thing sighted by the person on awakening.220

No magical water is administered to Felismena or Belisa, since both are of notable families and therefore "enlightened." Unlike the "unlearned" shepherds who must undergo a magical transformation in order to advance to a level of intellectual perception, Felismena and Belisa, already equipped with a measure of True Reason, and having enjoyed reciprocated affections, are left to solve their own amorous problems.221 For this, Felicia exorts Felismena to have faith in God (p. 223), complementing in this respect the Renaissance painters' interpretation of decorum as not only the suitable representation of typical aspects of human life, but also as specific conformity to what is proper in matters of morality and religion.

The next occurrence of altered affection is that of Felix. After Dórida, Felicia's nymph, has resuscitated the wounded knight sufficiently for him to understand her purpose, she addresses him with these words: "Cavallero, si queréis cobrar la vida y dalla a quien tan mala, a causa vuestra, [i.e., Felismena], la a passado, beved del agua deste vaso" (p. 297). Felix drinks from the golden flask and soon "se sintió tan sano de las heridas que los cavalleros le avían hecho y de la que amor, a causa de la señora Celia, le avía dado que no sentía más la pena que cada una dellas le podían causar que si nunca las uviera tenido. Y de tal manera se bolvió a renovar el amor de Felismena que en ningún tiempo le pareció aver estado tan vivo como entonces" (p. 297)

Felicia's redeeming action brings to mind Davis' interpretation of the action of pastoral romances. According to him, "...the standard action consists of these elements in this order: disintegration in the turbulent outer circle [the world of romance], education in the pastoral circle and rebirth at the sacred center."222 Such division of pastoral action complements Dante's theological division of human history into the era *ante legem*, the era *sub lege*, and the era *sub gratia*,223 which correspond symbolically and respectively in *Diana* to the state of the shepherds in their passion, in the realm of the "leyes" of the Temple of Diana, and in the enjoyment of grace received from Felicia's draught.

Following the example set by Dante's mentor, Virgil, Renaissance writers looked for meaning in the pastoral, and the earliest formal criticism of the genre, Sebillet's "L'Art poétique françoys" (1548) emphatically calls for the use of allegory in pastoral literature.[224] Like Alexander Barclay before him, Philip Sidney will later argue that the allegorical content gives pastoral the only value it has.[225] Allegory was a favorite tool of Renaissance man who "was passionately interested in everything secret and esoteric and studied all available models wherever he could find them."[226] This propensity to use the mysterious and to hide deep meanings[227] in it is certainly shared by Montemayor whose *Diana* is pervaded by a subtle play of meaning and double meaning.

At first Felicia's magical intervention seems to be merely a part of the conventional and often entertaining action of many romances that are built around a quest where the hero acquires some secret knowledge or magic object which aids him in overcoming obstacles along the way. We will remember how Lancelot, in search of Guinevere, gets a magic ring to protect him from hostile enchantments, and how a knight in Maria de France's ballad *Les Deus Amanz* is given a vial of potion by an old, learned, woman. The novelistic funcion of the magic draught in *Diana* has been the object of critical inquiry since the pronouncement made by the curate in *Don Quijote's* famous scrutiny of the library:[228] "y pues comenzamos por *La Diana* de Montemayor, soy de parecer que no se queme, sino que se le quite todo aquello que trata de la sabia Felicia y de la agua encantada" (*Quijote*, I, 6). Américo Castro defends the attitude expressed by Cervantes, noting that what the great Spanish novelist condemns is "la frivolidad del autor, para quien el impulso erótico, la esencia vital más poderosa, según Cervantes, puede cambiar de carácter y rumbo mediante un trago de agua."[229] Rather than "frivolity," the philter is a *deus ex machina* to Juan Bautista Avalle-Arce, who sees the water as easing plot developments hampered by the characters' inflexible attitude toward love (which stems from the Neoplatonic philosophy of the time).[230] It is in this context that T. Anthony Perry sees the wise Felicia as an "allegory" for the "desire and pursuit of happiness."[231] Significantly, as Gustavo Correa has noted, there is a certain psychological verisimilitude to the magic philter which turns grief into happiness. For Correa, the draught brings about a metamorphosis in the lovers through sleep which, "con su acción reparadora comporta un mecanismo intensificador del tiempo (olvido), que acorta los períodos de espera y presenta soluciones a los problemas de la imposibilidad."[232]

The magic philter, therefore, in addition to providing excitement and suspense, as is so often the case in romances of chivalry, serves as a symbolic vehicle for the passage of time; time, which in turn brings about a change in the lovers' attitude toward love.[233] In this respect, time serves as a "Revealer," known, as Erwin Panofsky points out "not only from many proverbs and poetical phrases, but also from countless representations of subjects such as Truth revealed or rescued by Time, Virtue vindicated by Time, Innocence justified by Time, and the like."[234] Thus, time, the destroyer of pastoral happiness, is also "the healer or wounds and producer of man's defense against sorrow, forgetfulness."[235] As the implications of the water of oblivion become clearer, so does the role of Felicia, whose portrayal finds a parallel of symbolic significance with the mythical god Anteros who, according to a legend ignored in the Middle Ages, but revived in the Renaissance, "was charged with the task of awakening in those who were loved 'love in return' or avenging all kinds of offenses against the god of love."[236] Similarly, the representation of Felicia as promoter of well-being finds an analogue in a tenth-century drawing of Apollo Medicus and in a fifteenth-century drawing representing Apollo the Healer. The Felicia-Apollo parallel is particularly revealing in terms of *Diana*-as-pilgrimage, for it is Orpheus, Apollo's son, who through his symbolic call for virtue prepares the shepherds for their redemption at the hands of Felicia.

The relationship of Felicia to Apollo is symbolically significant also if we bear in mind that Dante invokes Apollo at the beginning of *Paradise*, I, 13. In the drawing of Apollo the Healer, attributed to the Florentine painter Maso Finiguerra, Apollo is seen standing at a patient's bedside, holding a book in his left hand and a partially filled flask in his right hand. Looking like an Oriental magician in the act of resuscitating a dead person, the Apollo in Finiguerra's drawing has been associated with a "savior God, God of learned mysteries, God of life and of health-giving plants."[237] In this respect the picture in question has gained the reputation of being "the most typical example of the tradition of the heroes and sages that places profane and sacred history on the same plane."[238] The identification of Christ with pagan figures has been documented by an exciting discovery of one of the earliest Christian mosaics in the excavation of the Vatican cemetery under St. Peter's in the 1940's. Carefully examined by Marion Lawrence,[239] this decoration depicts what he convincingly interprets to be the figure of Christ-Helios "beardless as he appears in the catacombs, with girt tunic and flying mantle... Behind his head are heavenly rays, which, stressing the vertical and the horizontals, suggest a great cross, but rayed like the sun and far larger than any Christian halo. He ascends the heaven triumphant in a chariot drawn by white horses... all unlike the Ascension of Christ as we know it in early Cristian art..."[240]

Panofsky has stressed that the revival of classical motifs and classical themes is "only one aspect of the Renaissance movement in art."[241] Another equally important one is what he calls the "reinterpretation" of classical images, invested with new meaning and symbolism. Neoplatonic exegesis, which had presented such legendary figures as Apollo, Luna and Ceres "with hitherto undreamed-of possibilites of reconciliation between the Bible and mythology, had now so obscured the distinction between the two that Christian dogma no longer seemed acceptable in anything but an allegorical sense."[242] Marsilio Ficino, of Florence (1433-1499), the most influential of the Neoplatonists, firmly believed that complete harmony existed between Platonism and Christianity. In fact, he devoted most of his life to the elucidation of Christian doctrine by means of Platonic concepts, which he placed on a par with the authority of those of the New Testament. In the words of Leonard Grant, "Ficino quite literally believed that Plato's work was divinely inspired."[243]

In view of the above, it is not surprising, then, to find the wise Felicia in the role of a Christianized pagan god. Felicia's relationship to divinity intent on resurrecting the wayfaring shepherds from their spiritual death is strengthened by another parallel, this time with the figure of Crist himself holding in his hands a scroll, "no doubt the Book of Life,"[244] carved in the funeral chapel of the seventh-century French Bishop, the Venerable Agilbert, in a portrayal of the Last Judgment.

In a book by Philippe Ariès, *Western Attitudes Toward Death*, we are reminded that, according to the general eschatology of the early centuries of Christendom, the dead who had entrusted their bodies to the care of the Church "went to sleep like the seven sleepers of Ephesus (*pausantes, in somno pacis*) and were at rest (*requiescant*) until the day of the Second Coming, of the great return, when they would awaken in the heavenly Jerusalem, in other words in Paradise."[245] Similarly, the dead who were not members of the Church would not be awakened and would be abandoned "to a state of nonexistence" (*op. cit.*, p. 31).

Ariès' comments suggest certain important parallels with *Diana*. In the novel the only pastoral figure unworthy of admission into Felicia's palace is the shepherdess Diana, because of her lack of fortitude and constancy. Accordingly, she is deprived of the miraculous healing bestowed upon her deserving sylvan friends, and subsequently becomes an outcast to the novel's pastoral society. By contrast, the other shepherds and shepherdesses partake of the sleep of beatitude to such intensity that in the words of Felismena "si el descanso de estos pastores está en dormir, ellos lo hazen de manera que vivirán los más descansados del mundo" (p. 224). To which Felicia adds: "... dormirán sin que baste *ninguna persona* a despertallos" (p. 224, italics mine). The explicit reference to *ninguna persona* rather than the expected *nadie* dramatizes the exclusive role of Felicia as the sole entity capable of "resurrecting" the shepherds from their "sueño" the "sueño de la muerte" (p. 227), as Sylvano describes it. When awakened by the sage Lady Felicia with the book of knowledge the revived shepherds will symbolically triumph over death and become truly the happiest characters of the pleasance.

The view stressed by Montemayor in his treatise *Los trabajos de los reyes* that "la justicia no es cosa del hombre, sino de Dios"[246] may well lend support to the symbolic role of the wise Felicia, as a godly figure. Seen thus, Felicia is not a mere agent who intercedes between man and the divine,[247] she actually symbolizes the divine. In this context it is not "wizardry that saves man"[248] but an allegorical action of God. The characters are not "drugged with a new sense of optimism based on a denial of the nature and implications of their former agonies;"[249] they are rather metamorphosed into new beings by divine grace. In this context, it is interesting to note that it is characteristic of Montemayor's devotional poetry to "emphasize man's ultimate dependency on grace" as Bryant L. Creel has shown, and to represent "man as being helpless and abject without that grace."[250] As Montemayor exalts grace in his religious verses, so does Felicia extol the qualities of her miraculous water, which the distraught shepherds and shepherdesses drink with an attitude of reverence. The intervention of one of the nymphs, who restores Felix to reason by sprinkling him with a symbolic water of baptism, reinforces the exclusive power of grace. The combination of antique and scriptural subject matter in the treatment of Felicia's magic water links *Diana* further to the visual arts of the Renaissance in that painters of the time looked upon biblical and classical elements "almost as indispensable to good invention as a knowledge of antique sculpture to good design."[251]

Like a Eucharistic function, the redeeming action of Felicia is shrouded in mystery. Following his spiritual awakening Sireno simply acquiesces in the mystery: "—Yo estoy, discreta señora, satisfecho de lo que desseava entender y assí creo que lo estaré, según tu claro juyzio, de todo lo que quisiere saber de ti, aunque otro entendimiento era menester más abundante que el mío para alcançar lo mucho que tus palabras comprehenden" (pp. 198-199). The magic water, like grace, is an instrument of control, and symbolizes victory over passion. The strength and efficacy of the water makes the lovers insensitive to the external world, and in this the philter is analogous to the power of the sacraments to resist temptation. The philter, Felicia notes, "sabe desatar los ñudos que este perverso del amor haze" (p. 225). The symbolic significance of the liquid potion has been acutely perceived by T. Anthony Perry for whom the philter "signifies a desire to purge and renew, water washes away, liquefies the hardened configuration of our destinies, restores the feeling of infinite possibility."[252] Thus, at Felicia's palace, which Walter R. Davis would see as the novel's sacred center,[253] the characters undergo a process of rebirth. Spiritually regimented the characters become like the pious faithful, instruments of divine will in a way that brings to mind the biblical message: "He restores my health: he leads me in the path of righteousness for his name's sake" (Psalm 23:3).

In restoring grace, with the miraculous philter and a book symbolic of her wisdom, Felicia restores also the power of reason to the afflicted lovers. With the aid of the magic philter, the wise Felicia reestablishes the law of nature, and returns to the shepherds and shepherdesses "the power to see reality and to evaluate it correctly."[254] Significantly, when Sireno is awakened from his enchanted state, he arises "con todo su juizio" (p. 225) and becomes what he really is, "Sireno, the serene one."[255] The remedy for the soul lies in knowledge, and by imparting reason to the shepherds and shepherdesses, Felicia heals their mental suffering and spiritual anguish. The superior symbolic role of Felicia links *Diana* well to the novelty in painting which, in Poussin's words, "does not consist principally in a new subject, but in good and new disposition and expression, and thus the subject from being common and old becomes singular and new."[256]

Conclusion

In conclusion, music, along with poetic accomplishments, was a necessary part of the ideal lover of the Renaissance.[1] Consistent with Montemayor's renowned role as lover and his professional interest in music, as well as the exigencies of pastoral literature, *Diana* reverberates with the sound of shepherds' rebecs, pipes and a variety of other instruments, both rustic and courtly. Characters contemplate their idyllic surroundings and record their impression in song. Their words become sublimated through music.[2] Accordingly, all the poems set to music acquire a greater loftiness and transcendence with a mesmerizing effect on those who sing them, as well as on their audience.

To the humanists music was, first of all, poetry itself, "ogni forma di poesia," in the words of Nino Pirrotta, "che nasce e si distingue dall'espressione prosastica in quanto la parola si armonizza e accoglie proporzioni di durate, ricorrenze di accenti, accordi di rime, simmetrie di versi, di elementi metrici e di strofe, per non dire di quelle orchestrazioni di suoni e di cellule ritmiche 'que... pulcram faciunt armoniam compaginis.'"[3] Sung, poetry acquires an even greater musicality, drawing unto itself the attention of shepherds. Let us remember that in all instances it is not what is sung that attracts the attention of the rustics of *Diana*, but rather the voice, the human sound.[4] The fact that Montemayor's shepherds sing also without musical accompaniment reflects the importance given by the author to the human voice.

In *Diana* the propensity to lament is equalled only by the shepherds' love of song and music. Musical elements skillfully interwoven in *Diana* with such theatrical aspects as scenery, costumes, and stage effects, ingeniously displayed in a frequently dramatic action, suggest an embryonic operatic form. In view of this, it appears that it would not be unreasonable to see Montemayor in the movement of musical currents of the time as opera developed in the direction of what the French writer Romain Rolland has called *L'Opéra avant l'Opéra*,[5] the operatic journey from Angelo Poliziano (*Orfeo*, 1480) through Ottavio Rinuccini (*Euridice*, 1600), and then to Claudio Monteverdi's grand "favola in musica," *Orfeo* (1607).

Montemayor, singer, musician, poet, novelist, and author of a book on heraldry, who lived much of his life in courtly circles, had access to many works of art, ancient and modern, and was unquestionably inspired by them, as he was by the stories of myth and legend that served as models to both literature and the visual arts. Furthermore, his travels to England, France, the Netherlands and northern Italy exposed him to well-known painters of the time, artists whom he surely respected and admired, as is evidenced by the fact that *Diana* illustrates with words their pictures, thereby paying tribute to them. One result of Montemayor's long and varied association with the arts is a novel in which every major event finds a corresponding representation in the visual arts, exemplifying several interesting analogies between poetry and painting, as discussed by Aristotle and Horace, who taught that painting, like poetry, is an imitation of human action of more than common beauty or significance, exactly as it occurs in *Diana*. Indeed, the very text of *Diana* invites us to read it as a visual experience. A highly descriptive style abounding in brilliant pictorial imagery and a lexicon that throbs with such words as "mirava" (p. 21), "veis" (p. 57), "vean" (p. 85), "veo" (p. 145), "mirando" (p. 181), "mirad" (p. 181), and "pinta" (p. 17), underscores the novelist's delight in visual artistic correspondences.

Notes to the Introduction

[1] Isabel Pope, "La vihuela y su música en el ambiente humanístico," *Nueva Revista de Filología Hispánica*, 15 (1961), 364-365. I wish to express my gratitude to Mr. Frederick D. Phillips, technical adviser to STUDIA HUMANITATIS, and Dr. Richard Sherr, Professor of Music at Smith College, for their careful reading of the present study and for their valuable suggestions.

[2] Miguel de Fuenllana, *Libro de música para vihuela intitulado "Orphénica lyra"* (Seville, 1554), cited by Isabel Pope, *op. cit.*, p. 365.

[3] Adolfo Salazar, *La música en Cervantes y otros ensayos* (Madrid: Insula, 1961), p. 137.

[4] Edward E. Lowinsky, *Secret Chromatic Art in the Netherlands Motet*, trans. Carl Buchman (New York: Russell and Russell, 1967), p. XVII.

[5] See Archivo de Simancas: Casa Real, leg. 44-50, 74; cf. Narciso Alonso Cortés, "Sobre Montemayor y *La Diana*," *Boletín de la Real Academia Española* 17 (1930), 353. See also, Higinio Anglés, *La Música en la Corte de Carlos V* (Barcelona, 1944), p. 78; cf. Jaime Moll, "La Princesa Juana de Austria y la música: notas para su estudio," *Anuario Musical*, 19 (1966), p. 1.

[6] A view attributed to Michaëlis de Vasconcellos; see Gustav Gröber's *Grundriss der romanischen Philologie* (Strassbourg: K.J. Trübner, 1894), II, 304, a work in which Michaëlis de Vasconcellos collaborated.

[7] Bryant Lawrence Creel, "The Religious Poetry of Jorge de Montemayor." (Ph.D. diss., University of California, Davis, 1978), p. 102. Montemayor's three *autos* were written for presentation before Philip II when he was still a prince, during the Christmas festivities of 1547 or of the preceding two years. They were published in Montemayor's *Obras* (Antwerp, 1554). See *El cancionero del poeta George de Montemayor* (Madrid: Sociedad de Bibliófilos Españoles, 1932), pp. 246-280, especially pp. 277-280.

[8] This poem is reproduced in the excellent edition of the *Poesias de Francisco de Sâ de Miranda* by Caroline Michaëlis de Vasconcellos (Halle, 1885, p. 655), and more recently by Marcial José Bayo, *Virgilio y la pastoral española del renacimiento* (Madrid: Gredos, 1959), p. 239.

[9] Judith M. Kennedy, *A Critical Edition of Yong's Translation of*

George of Montemayor's Diana and Gil Polo's Enamoured Diana (London: Oxford University Press, 1968), p. XV.

[10] Higinio Anglés, *op. cit.*, p. 83.

[11] Gustave Reese, *Music in the Renaissance* (New York: W.W. Norton, 1959), p. 395.

[12] Salazar, *op. cit.*, p. 129.

[13] Cf. Gustave Reese, *op. cit.*, p. 627.

[14] Federico Sopeña, "La música española," *Cuadernos Hispanoamericanos*, 58 (1964), 313.

[15] Erwin Panofsky, *Problems in Titian* (New York University Press, 1969), p. 125.

[16] Gustave Reese, *op. cit.*, p. 568.

[17] Adolfo Salazar, *op. cit.*, p. 128.

[18] Higinio Anglés, *op. cit.*, pp. 12ff.

[19] Thomas G. Rosenmeyer, *The Green Cabinet. Theocritus and the European Pastoral Novel* (Berkeley, 1969), p. 166.

[20] A quality attributed to stringed instruments by Edwin Panofsky, *Problems in Titian* (New York University Press, 1969), p. 125.

[21] Eleanor Terry Lincoln, ed. *Pastoral and Romance. Modern Essays in Criticism* (Englewood Cliffs, N.J.: Prentice Hall, 1969), p. 2.

[22] Leonardo da Vinci, *Trattato della pintura*, discussed by A.P. McMahon, *Leonardo da Vinci, Treatise on Painting* (Princeton, 1956), p. 25.

[23] Erwin Panofsky, *op. cit.*, p. 120.

[24] Marsilio Ficino, *In Convivium Platonis Commentarium*, I, *Opera omnia*, pp. 1322ff.; see Paul Oskar Kristeller, *The Philosophy of Marsilio Ficino*, p. 37; cited in Erwin Panofsky, *op. cit.*, p. 1.

[25] Bruce W. Wardropper, "The *Diana* of Montemayor: Revaluation and Interpretation," *Studies in Philology*, 48 (1951). 132.

[26] Enrique Moreno Báez, ed. *Los siete libros de la Diana* (Madrid: Editorial Nacional, 1976), p. xviii.

Notes to Chapter I

[1] Pedrell, *Organografía*, pp. 52, 56, 97, cited by Miguel Querol Gavaldá, *La música en la obras de Cervantes* (Barcelona: Comtalia, 1948), p. 138.

[2] Howard Mayer Brown, *Sixteenth Century Instrumentation: The Music for the Florentine Intermedii* (New York: American Institute of Musicology, 1973), p. 49.

[3] Thomas G. Rosenmeyer, *op. cit.*, p. 166.

[4] Francesco Petrarca, *Rime, Trionfi e poesie latine* (Milan, 1951), p. 26, XXIII, Canzone I.

[5] R.G. Keightley, "Narrative Perspectives in Spanish Pastoral Fiction," *Journal of the Australasian Universities Language and Literature Association*, 44 (1975), 194-219.

[6] Cf. Miguel Querol Gavaldá, *op. cit.*, p. 149.

[7] Howard Mayer Brown, *op. cit.*, p. 12.

[8] See, for instance, accounts of the *intermedii* performed in honor of Medici weddings, in Andrew C. Minor and Bonner Mitchell, eds., *A Renaissance Entertainment* (Columbia: University of Missouri Press, 1968), and D.P. Walker, ed., *Les Fêtes du mariage de Ferdinand de Médicis et de Christine de Lorraine*, Florence 1589, Vol. I: *Musique des Intermèdes* de "La Pellegrina" (Paris: Centre national de la recherche scientifique, 1963). Particularly useful for a general history of the intermedio is Nino Pirrotta, "Intermedium," *Die Musik in Geschichte und Gegenwart*, 6 (1957), cols. 1310-26. See also Pirrotta, *Li Due Orfei da Poliziano a Monteverdi* (Turin, Edizioni RAI, 1969).

[9] Donald Jay Grout, *A Short History of Opera* (New York and London: Columbia University Press, 1965), p. 23.

[10] Howard Mayer Brown, *op. cit.*, p. 11. See also, Emilie Elsner, *Untersuchung der instrumentalen Besetzungspraxis der weltlichen Musik im 16. Jahrhundert in Italien* (Ohlau i. Schl.: Eschenhagen, 1935).

[11] *Ibid.*, p. 12.

[12] In the sixteenth century, the Spanish word for "clavichord" was "manocordio." See Raymond Russell, *The Harpsichord and Clavichord: An Introductory Study* (London: Faber and Faber, 1959), p. 116.

[13] Miguel Querol Gavaldá, *op. cit.*, p. 35.

[14] Gustave Reese, *op. cit.*, p. 631.
[15] Isabel Pope, *op. cit.*, p. 369.
[16] *Ibid.*
[17] *Ibid.*, pp. 366-367.
[18] Miguel de Fuenllana, *Orphénica lyra*, cited in Isabel Pope, *op. cit.*, p. 365.
[19] Adolfo Salazar, *op. cit.*, pp. 130-131, note 4.
[20] Gustave Reese, *op. cit.*, p. 614.
[21] Alonso de Mudarra, *Tres libros de música en cifra para vihuela* (Seville, 1546). Transcriptions and study by Emilio Puyol (Barcelona, 1949), p. 155.
[22] Cf. Antonio della Torre, *Storia dell'Accademia Platonica di Firenze* (Florence, 1902), 788 ff., and Paul Oskar Kristeller, *The Philosophy of Marsilio Ficino* (New York, 1943).
[23] *The Book of the Courtier*, trans. Charles S. Singleton (New York: Doubleday, 1959), pp. 104-105, and 362-363, n. 4 and 5.
[24] Gustave Reese, *op. cit.*, p. 160, n. 49.
[25] *Ibid.*
[26] Edward E. Lowinsky, "Music in Renaissance Culture," *Renaissance Essays from the Journal of the History of Ideas*, ed. Oskar Kristeller and Philip P. Wiener (New York: Harper and Row, 1968), p. 344.
[27] Salazar, *op. cit.*, p. 200.
[28] Gustave Reese, *op. cit.*, p. 667.
[29] *Ibid.*, p. 529.
[30] Salazar, *op. cit.*, p. 279.
[31] Gustave Reese, *op. cit.*, p. 529.
[32] *Ibid.*, p. 561.
[33] *Ibid.*, p. 558.
[34] *Ibid.*, p. 561.
[35] *Ibid.*, p. 559.
[36] Higinio Anglés, *op. cit.*, pp. 13 ff.
[37] Salazar, *op. cit.*, p. 295, n. 38.
[38] Miguel Querol Gavaldá, *op. cit.*, p. 154.
[39] *Ibid.*, p. 156.
[40] Isabel Pope, *Cancionero de Upsala* (Mexico, 1944), p. 15.
[41] Henry Pleasants, *The Great Singers from the Dawn of Opera to Our Own Time*, (New York: Simon and Schuster, 1966), p. 24.
[42] Salazar, *op. cit.*, p. 138.
[43] *Disput. Tusc.* V. 22.

44In Alonso Mudarra's dedicatory epistle to Luis Zapata, as cited by Isabel Pope, *op. cit.*, p. 365.
45In Gonzalo de Berceo (*Duelo de la Virgen*) we read: "controbando cantares que non valian tres figas / tocando intrumentos cedras, rotas e gigas / cantaban los trufanes unas controbaduras" (cited by Adolfo Salazar, *op. cit.*, p. 249).
46Salazar, *op. cit.*, p. 249.
47*Ibid.*, p. 158.
48Henry Pleasants, *op. cit.*, p. 42.
49Angus Heriot, *The Castrati in Opera*, (New York: Da Capo Press, 1974), pp. 36-37.
50See Richard Sherr, "Guglielmo Gonzaga and the Castrati," *Renaissance Quarterly*, 30 (1980), 33-56. Cf. Angus Heriot, *op. cit.*, pp. 11, 15.
51*Ibid.*, p. 13.
52Edward E. Lowinsky, *op. cit.*, p. 349.
53Salazar, *op. cit.*, p. 251.
54Howard Mayer Brown, *op. cit.*, p. 27.
55Salazar, *op. cit.*, p. 379.
56See Karl Weinmann, *Johannes Tinctoris (1445-1511) und sein unbekannter Traktat "De inventione et usu musicae."* Regensburg-Rome, 1917. English translation by Anthony Baines, "Fifteenth-Century Instruments in Tinctoris's *De inventione et usu musicae*," *The Galpin Society Journal*, 3 (March, 1950), 19-26.
57Higinio Anglés, *op. cit.*, pp. 1-141, particularly p. 7.
58The first Italian collections of music for lute were the books of *Frottole* published in Venice by Ottaviano de' Petrucci, Francesco Spinaccino (1507), Giovanni Ambrosio d'Alza (1508) and Franciscus Bossinensis (1509).
59Miguel Querol Gavaldá, *op. cit.*, p. 141.
60Adolfo Salazar, *op cit.*, p. 378.
61*Ibid.*, p. 342.
62Miguel Querol Gavaldá, *op. cit.*, p. 144.
63See Baldesar Castiglione, *The Book of the Courtier*, ed. cit., pp. 45, 60, 74-76; 104.
64The others are the lyre, cithern, plectrum, vihuela, lute and guitar; see Pablo Cabañas, *El mito de Orfeo en la literatura española* (Madrid: Consejo Superior de Investigaciones Científicas, 1948), p. 89.

65Marqués de Santillana, *Obras*, ed. Amador de los Ríos (Madrid, 1902), p. 423.
66Juan de Mena, *Laberinto de Fortuna* (Madrid, 1934), p. 27.
67Fernando de Rojas, *La Celestina*, ed. Julio Cejador y Frauca (Madrid, 1947), II, 231, cited in Pablo Cabañas, *op. cit.*, p. 106.
68Michael Grant, "The Myth of Orpheus and Eurydice," in *History Today*, June, 1967, p. 372.
69*Ibid.*
70*Ibid.*
71Peter V. Marinelli, *Pastoral* (London: Methuen, 1971), p. 49.
72Salazar, *op. cit.*, p. 65.
73Edward Lowinsky, *op. cit.*, p. 357.
74Rosenmeyer, *op. cit.*, p. 152.
75*Ibid.*, p. 157.
76Emilio Cotarelo y Mori, *Historia de la Zarzuela* (Madrid, 1934), p. 36.
77Elias L. Rivers, "The Pastoral Paradox of Natural Art," *Modern Language Notes*, 77 (1962), p. 144.
78J. Anthony Perry, "Ideal Love and Human Reality in Montemayor's *La Diana*," *Publications of the Modern Languages Association*, 84 (1969), 277.
79Enrique Moreno Báez, ed. *Los siete libros de la Diana* (Madrid: Nacional, 1976), XLIII.
80*Ibid.*, p. XLII.
81Cassiodorus, *De Musica*, cited by Miguel Querol Gavaldá, *op. cit.*, p. 28.
82Edward E. Lowinsky, *op. cit.*, p. 350.
83Baldesar Castiglione *The Book of the Courtier, ed. cit.*, p. 75.
84Music and its effects in *Diana* is discussed briefly and quite superficially by Francisco López Estrada, "Las Bellas Artes en relación con la concepción estética de la novela pastoril," *Anales de la Universidad Hispalense*, 14 (1953), pp. 66-70.
85Rosenmeyer, *op. cit.*, p. 152.
86Marcelino Menéndez y Pelayo, *Orígenes de la novela* (Santander: Consejo Superior de Investigaciones Científicas, 1943), II, 276.
87RoseAnna M. Mueller, "Montemayor's *Diana*: A Translation

and introduction." (Ph.D. diss., City University of New York, 1977), p. 19.

[88]*La rappresentazione di anima, et di corpo novamente posta in musica dal sig. Emilio del Cavaliere per recitar cantando* cited in Nino Pirrotta, *Li due Orfei: Da Poliziano a Monteverdi* (Torino: Einaudi, 1975), p. 280.

[89]Mary Gay Doman, "Patterns of Sentence Structure in *La Diana, De los Nombres de Cristo* and *Menosprecio de corte y alabanza de aldea*. A Transformational Linguistic Approach to Stylistic Analysis." (Ph.D. diss., University of Wisconsin-Madison, 1976), p. 76.

[90]Emilio Náñez, "El adjectivo en la Galatea," *Anales Cervantinos*, 4 (1957), 147; cited by Mary Gay Doman, *op. cit.*, p. 76. Cf. Francisco López Estrada, ed. *Diana* (Madrid: Espasa Calpe, 1953), p. lxxv.

[91]Mary Gay Doman, *op. cit.*, p. 76.

[92]Cf. Francisco López Estrada, *La "Galatea" de Cervantes* (La Laguna de Tenerife, 1948), p. 127.

[93]Donald Jay Grout, *A Short History of Opera* (New York and London: Columbia University Press, 1965), p. 32.

Notes to Chapter II

[1] Textual references to *Diana* are based on the edition of Francisco López Estrada, Madrid: Clásicos Castellanos, 1945.
[2] See Leonardo da Vinci's *Notebooks*, trans. by Edward McCurdy (Garden City, N.Y.: Garden City Publishing Company, 1941), pp. 156-160; Moritz Thausing, *Albrecht Dürer, His Life and Works*, (London: J. Murray, 1882), p. 319. Francisco de Olanda, "Third Dialogue on Painting," in Charles Holroyd, *Michelangelo Buonarroti* (London: Duckworth, 1903), p. 322.
[3] Thomas G. Rosenmeyer, *The Green Cabinet: Theocritus and the European Pastoral Lyric* (Berkeley, 1969), p. 135.
[4] *Ibid.*, p. 133.
[5] Shown in "A Sixteenth Century Farmer's Year," *History Today*, June 1970, p. 399.
[6] Thomas G. Rosenmeyer, *op. cit.*, p. 143.
[7] Cited by Emilio Orozco Díaz, *Paisaje y sentimiento de la naturaleza en la poesía española* (Madrid: Prensa Española, 1968), p. 116.
[8] Francisco de Olanda, *Quatro diálogos sobre a pintura* (Porto, 1896), p. 96.
[9] Ludovico Dolce, *Dialogo della pittura intitolato l'Aretino* (Florence, 1735 [first ed. Venice, 1557]), p. 116. See Rensselaer W. Lee, "Ut pictura poesis: The Humanistic Theory of Painting," *The Art Bulletin*, 22 (1940), 197-263.
[10] Leon Battista Alberti, *Della pittura* (1436), cited in Rensselaer W. Lee, *op. cit.*, p. 219.
[11] Giovanni Paolo Lomazzo, *Trattato dell'arte della pittura, scoltura, et architettura* (Milan, 1585), II, 1, p. 105.
[12] Leonardo da Vinci, *Trattato della pittura*, discussed in Lee, *op. cit.*, p. 219.
[13] *Laokoön*, translated by Robert Philimore (London, 1874), p. 141.
[14] *Trattato III*, 377; cited by Rensselaer W. Lee, *op. cit.*, p. 230.
[15] Thomas G. Rosenmeyer, *op. cit.*, p. 239.
[16] *Medals*, George Francis Hill, *A Corpus of Italian Medals in the British Museum* (London: British Museum, 1930), p. 661. Henceforth referred to as *Medals*.
[17] *Q. Horatii Flacci Opera*, ed. J.B. Lechatellier (Paris: Gigord, 1937), p. 48.

[18] Enrique Moreno Báez, *ed. cit.*, p. xxviii.
[19] Cf. Jesús Cutiérrez, *La "Fortuna Bifrons" en el teatro del Siglo de Oro* (Santander: Sociedad Menéndez Pelayo, 1975), p. 15.
[20] Joseph R. Jones, "'Human Time' in *La Diana*," *Romance Notes*, 10 (1968), 140.
[21] Amadeu Solé-Leris, *The Spanish Pastoral Novel* (Boston: G.K. Hall, 1980), p. 38.
[22] Shown in *Catalogue of Images of Love and Death in Late Medieval and Renaissance Art*. Essays by Clifton C. Olds, Ralph G. Williams; Catalogue by William R. Levin, The University of Michigan, Museum of Art, November 21, 1975, to January 4, 1976. Plate XLIII.
[23] *Medals*, pp. 137, 532.
[24] See Ruth El Saffar, "Structural and Thematic Discontinuity in Montemayor's *Diana*," *Modern Language Notes*, 86 (1971), 187.
[25] The painting, now at the Louvre, is discussed in Erwin Panofsky, *Problems in Titian* (New York University Press, 1969), pp. 91-92; it is also reproduced in figure 108.
[26] *Ibid.*, p. 93.
[27] *Ibid.*
[28] *Ibid.*, p. 92.
[29] R. Wittkower, *Gian Lorenzo Bernini*, 2nd ed. (London, 1966), p. 211f., Fig. 56, 57.
[30] Renato Poggioli, "The Pastoral of the Self," in *Daedalus*, 88 (1959), 699.
[31] See. E. Rohde, *Der griechische Roman und seine Vorläufer* (Leipzig, 1876), p. 44, and W.H. Roscher, *Ausführliches Lexikon de grieshischen und römischen Mythologie* (Leipzig, 1886-90), I, 2800-2803.
[32] Walter Friedlaender, "Hymenaeus," in *De Artibus Opuscula XL. Essays in Honor of Erwin Panofsky*, ed. Millard Meiss (New York University Press, 1961), I, 153-56. The painting is reproduced in vol. II, p. 52.
[33] *Ibid.*, p. 154.
[34] *Ibid.*, p. 156.
[35] Albert Guérard, *Literature and Society* (New York: Cooper Square, 1970), p. 62.
[36] This motif came to be very common in Roman poetry as A. Kiessling and R. Heinze note in their *Q. Horatius Flaccus, Oden und Epoden* (Berlin, 1917), p. 345; see *Odes* 3.18.

37Francisco López Estrada, *Los libros de pastores en la literatura española* (Madrid: Gredos, 1974), p. 518.
38Dámaso Alonso and José Manuel Blecua, *Antología de la poesía española. Lirica de tipo tradicional*, 2nd ed. (Madrid, 1964), p. 32, n. 64; p. 41, n. 80; p. 49, n. 104; p. 80, n. 221; p. 176, n. 406; p. 74, n. 175; p. 90, n. 221; p. 198, n. 446; p. 82, n. 205. The social background of these poems is discussed briefly by F. López Estrada, *Los libros de pastores*, pp. 281-92.
39F. López Estrada, *Los libros de pastores*, p. 293.
40Shown in Walter Salmen, *Musikleben im 16. Jahrhundert*; Band III: Musik des Mittelalters und der Renaissance. Lfg, 9 (VEB Deutscher Verlag für Musik, Leipzig, 1976), Abbildung 2, p. 57.
41In Salmen,*op. cit.*, Abbildung 14, p. 65.
42See Florence Whyte, "Three *Autos* of Jorge de Montemayor," *Publications of The Modern Languages Association*, 43 (1928), 953-989.
43Michael J. Woods, *The Poet and the Natural World in the Age of Góngora* (London: Oxford University Press), 1978, p. 164.
44*Ibid.*, p. 108.
45Marcelin Defourneaux, *Daily Life in Spain in the Golden Age*, trans. Newton Branch (New York: Praeger, 1970), p. 128.
46*Ibid.*, p. 129.
47*La gran sultana*, cited by Ludwig Pfandl, *Cultura y costumbres del pueblo español de los siglos* XVI y XVII. *Siglo de Oro* (Barcelona: Araluce, 1929), p. 250, n.
48Michael Squires, *op. cit.*, p. 119.
49Marcelin Defourneaux, *op. cit.*, p. 129.
50Baldesar Castiglione, *Book of the Courtier*, trans. Charles S. Singleton (New York: Doubleday, 1959), p. 103.
51Howard Mayer Brown, *Sixteenth Century Instrumentation: The Music for the Florentine Intermedii* (American Institute of Musicology, 1973), p. 12.
52Adolfo Salazar, *La música en la sociedad española* (Mexico, 1942), I, 251.
53Howard Mayer Brown, *op cit.*, p. 49.
54Higinio Anglés, *La música en la corte de Carlos V* (Barcelona, 1944), p. 12ff.
55In book illustration of c. 1590, reproduced in Salmen, *op. cit.*, Abbildung 84, p. 133.

[56] Shown in George Kinsky, *A History of Music in Pictures* (New York: Dutton, 1930), p. 122.
[57] Montagu, *op. cit.*, p. 34, Plate 32.
[58] *Ibid.*
[59] Jeremy Montagu, *World of Medieval and Renaissance Musical Instruments* (Woodstock, N.J.: Overlook Press, 1976), p. 67, Plate 52.
[60] Shown in Emanuel Winternitz, *Musical Instruments and Their Symbolism in Western Art* (London: Faber, 1967).
[61] Montagu, *op. cit.*, p. 105, Plate 77; p. 106, Plate 78.
[62] Jost Aman, "Ehebrecherbrücke des Königs Artus," shown in Alexander Buchner, *Musical Instruments: An Illustrated History* (New York: Crown Publishers 1973), p. 26.
[63] *Medals*, pp. 257, 973.
[64] Antonio Minturno, *L'Amore innamorato* (Venice: F. Rampazeto, 1559), pp. 4-5. This work received adequate attention from Francisco López Estrada, "*L'amore innamorato* de Minturno (1559) y su repercusión en la literatura pastoril española," in *Homenaje a Joaquín Casalduero*, ed. Rizel Pincus Sigele y Gonzalo Sobejano (Madrid: Gredos, 1972), pp. 315-324.
[65] Cf. "Relation du voyage frère Bieul," in *L'Extreme Orient au Moyen Age*, ed. Louis de Backer (Paris, 1877), p. 257.
[66] The comment made by Oskar Kristeller, *The Philosophy of Marsilio Ficino*, p. 112, cited in Erwin Panofsky, *Problems in Titian*, p. 119.
[67] Erwin Panofsky, *Problems in Titian*, p. 114.
[68] *Ibid.*
[69] *Ibid.*, p. 115.
[70] Shown in Richard Bernheimer, *Wild Men in the Middle Ages: A Study in Art, Sentiment and Demonology* (Cambridge, Harvard University Press, 1952), Plate 28.
[71] Thomas Rosenmeyer, *op. cit.*, p. 59.
[72] *Palmerín de Inglaterra*, ed. A. Bonilla y San Martín, *Nueva Biblioteca de Autores Españoles*, XI, 52.
[73] Diego de San Pedro, *Obras*, ed. S. Gili y Gaya (Madrid: Clásicos Castellanas, 1950), p. 116.
[74] A concise but useful summary of the role of the *salvaje* in literature and art is given by José A Madrigal, *op. cit.* See also, Richard Bernheimer, *Wild Men in the Middle Ages* (Cambridge, Mass., 1952) and José M. de Azcárate, "El tema iconográfico del salvaje," *Archivo Español de Arte*, 31 (1948), 81-89.

[75] Bruce W. Wardropper, *op. cit.*, p. 130. See, also, Oleh Mazur, "Various Folkloric Impacts upon the Salvaje in the Spanish Comedia," *Hispanic Review*, 36 (1968), 219.

[76] Cf. Pomponius Mela, *De Situ Orbis*, Ex typographia societatis Bipontinae (n.p., 1809), p. 86. See K. Müller, *Geographia Graeci Minores* (Paris, 1855), p. xviii; William Coffman McDermott, *The Ape in Antiquity* (Baltimore: The Johns Hopkins University Studies in Archaelogy n. 27 [1938]), 69.

[77] Cf. Oleh Mazur, *op. cit.*, p. 233.

[78] Shown in Norman Cohn, "Monsters of Chaos," *Horizon*, Autumn, 1972, p. 47.

[79] *Medals*, p. 72.

[80] José María de Azcárate, "El tema iconográfico del salvaje," *Archivo Español del Arte*, 21 (1948), 81-99.

[81] See Hugh Clark, *An Introduction to Heraldry* (London: Washbourne, 1854), plate H 24.

[82] See Gysin Frédéric, *Tapisseries suisses de l'époque gothique* (Bâle, 1947), figs. VII and ff.

[83] Cf. José M. de Azcárate, *op. cit.*, p. 98.

[84] See Enrique del Castillo, *Crónica de Enrique IV* in *Biblioteca de Autores Españoles*, 70, chapter XXIV, p. 113.

[85] Bierens de Haan, *Het Hontsnijwerk im Nederland tijdens de Gothic en de Renaissance* (D. Gravenhage, 1921), figs. 60, 61.

[86] See José M. de Azcárate, *op. cit.*, p. 93.

[87] Richard Bernheimer, *Wild Men in the Middle Ages* (Cambridge, 1952), p. 56.

[88] James M. Clark, *The Dance of Death in the Middle Ages and the Renaissance* (Glasgow, 1950), p. 31.

[89] E.H. Langlois, A. Pottier, Alfred Bandry, *Essai historique philosophique et pittoresque sur les Danses des Morts, suivi d'une lettre de M.C. Leber et d'une note de M. Depping sur le même sujet* (Rouen, 1851), p. 298.

[90] Cf. Richard Bernheimer, *op. cit.*, p. 50.

[91] *Ibid.*, p. 51.

[92] *Ibid.*

[93] *Ibid.*, p. 62.

[94]*Ibid.*, p. 69.
[95]Morris Bishop, "The World of Froissart," in *Horizon*, Autumn, 1972, p. 76.
[96]James M. Clark, *op. cit.*, pp. 92-93.
[97]An intelligent explanation of the meaning and significance of this expression within the context of pastoral literature and art is given by Erwin Panofsky, "Et in Arcadia ego," in *Pastoral and Romance: Modern Essays in Criticism*, ed. Eleanor Terry Lincoln (Englewood Cliffs, N.J.: Prentice Hall, 1969), pp. 25-46.
[98]Shown in Hugh Clark, *An Introduction to Heraldry* (London: Washbourne, 1854), Plate H 22, X.
[99]Robert Graves, *The Greek Myths* (Baltimore, 1955), I, 167; 18, 81. See Michael Levey, *A Short History of Painting from Giotto to Cézanne* (Toronto, New York: Oxford University Press, 1962), Plate 52, p. 38.
[100]Study submitted to *Hispanic Review*.
[101]Jorge de Montemayor, *Exposición moral sobre el salmo LXXXVI del real propheta David* (Alcalá de Henares, 1548), republished by Francisco López Estrada, "La exposición moral sobre el salmo LXXXVI de Jorge de Montemayor," *Revista de Bibliografía Nacional*, 5 (1944), 499-523.
[102]Quoted in Erwin Panofsky, *Studies in Iconology: Humanistic Themes in the Art of the Renaissance* (New York: Oxford University Press, 1939), p. 70.
[103]Américo Castro, "Lo hispánico y el erasmismo," *Revista de Filología Hispánica*, 4 (1942), 58.
[104]Rensselaer W. Lee, *op. cit.*, p. 203.
[105]Erwin Panofsky, *Problems in Titian*, p. 86. See, also, A. Alföldi, "*Hasta-Summa Imperii*; The Spear as Embodiment of Sovereignty in Rome," *American Journal of Archaeology*, 63 (1959), ff. Cf. Lynn White, Jr. *Medieval Technology and Social Change* (New York, 1973), p. 151.
[106]Reproduced in Priscilla Flood, "*Les Belles Heures* of the Duc de Berry," *Horizon*, Autumn, 1974, p. 71.

[107] Leon Battista Alberti, *Della pittura*, 1436, cited by Rensselaer W. Lee, *op. cit.*, p. 201.

[108] The picture is shown in Jean Seznec, *The Survival of the Pagan Gods* (New York: Pantheon, 1953), p. 111.

[109] Francisco Márquez Villanueva, "Las joyas de Felismena," *Revue de littérature comparée*, 52 (1978), 269-277.

[110] Márquez Villanueva (*op. cit.*, p. 269) cites a most useful bibliography to substantiate this point, including the very informative study of Gaspar de Morales, *Libro de las virtudes y propiedades maravillosas de las piedras preciosas* (Madrid: Blas Gonçález, 1605), f. 201v.

[111] Márquez Villanueva, *op. cit.*, p. 269.

[112] Harold Bayley, *A New Light on the Renaissance Displayed in Contemporary Emblems* (London: J.M. Dent, 1909), p. 255.

[113] The point is well presented and amply documented by Márquez Villanueva (*op. cit.*, p. 270), who recalls the use made of the symbolic *barquillas* by Lope de Vega in his *La Dorotea*; cf. Edwin S. Morby, "A footnote on Lope de Vega's *Barquillas*," *Romance Philology*, 6 (1953), 289-293.

[114] These observations are made by Márquez Villanueva, *op. cit.*, p. 271.

[115] Gaspar de Morales, *Libros de las virtudes*, f. 101v and 103v, cited by Márquez Villanueva, *op. cit.*, p. 272, n. 26.

[116] Gaspar de Morales, *op. cit.*, f. 40v, also cited by Márquez Villanueva, *op. cit.*, p. 272, n. 25.

[117] Márquez Villanueva, *op. cit.*, p. 271.

[118] Márquez Villanueva cites the symbolic value of the pearl as used by, among others, Raban Mauro and Dante, the latter comparing it to the active souls of Paradise (*op. cit.*, p. 271).

[119] Cf. John W. Beatty, *The Relation of Art to Nature* (New York: Wm. Edwin Rudge, 1922), p. 16.

[120] The sapphire has also been found to be a "conspicuous symbol of hope;" see Márquez Villanueva (*op. cit.*, p. 272) who cites examples from a French medieval poet and Dante (*Purgatorio*, I, 13).

[121]Emilio Orozco Díaz, *Amor, poesía y pintura en Carrillo de Sotomayor* (Granada, 1967), p. 37.

[122]Harold Bayley, *op. cit.*, p. 25.

[123]*Ibid.*

[124]See Arthur Henkel and Albrecht Schöne, *Emblemata* (Stuttgart, 1967), cols. 652-59, and G. de Tervarent, *Les énigmes de l'art. L'héritage antique* (Paris, 1946), cols. 340-42. Both works mentioned by Márquez Villanueva, *op. cit.*, p. 275, n. 40.

[125]E. Ingersoll, *Birds in Legend, Tale and Folklore* (New York, 1923), p. 150, referred to by Márquez Villanueva, *op. cit.*, p. 275, n. 41.

[126]Márquez Villanueva, *op. cit.*, p. 275.

[127]*Ibid.*, p. 276.

[128]This view is expressed by Márquez Villanueva (*op. cit.*, p. 276) who echoes the observations made by Bruce Wardropper, *op. cit.*, p. 41, and Antonio A. Cirurgião, "O papel da beleza na *Diana* de Jorge de Montemor," *Hispania*, 51 (1968), 402-7.

[129]Mario Praz, *Studies in Seventeenth Century Imagery*. Rome, 1964.

[130]Karl Ludwig Selig, "The Spanish Translation of Alciato's Emblemata," in *Modern Language Notes*, 70 (1955), 354-359.

[131]Francisco Márquez Villavueva, *op. cit.*, p. 273.

[132]See M. Bacci, *Piero di Cosimo* (Milan, 1966), pp. 67-8.

[133]Irving Stone "The Perfect Beauty," *Horizon*, September, 1958, Vol. I, N. 1, p. 93.

[134]*Medals*, p. 273.

[135]Marc F. Bertonasco, *Crashaw and the Baroque* (University of Alabama, 1971), p. 31, cited by Frederick de Armas, "Las tres Dianas de Montemayor," "*Lingüística y Educación. Actas del IV Congreso Internacional de la ALFAL* (Lima, 1978), p. 190.

[136]Frederick A. de Armas, *op. cit.*, p. 190.

[137]Jorge de Montemayor, *Libro de blasones*, cited by Domingo García Peres, *op. cit.*, *Catálogo razonado biográfico y bibliográfico de los autores portugueses que escribieron en castellano* (Madrid, 1890), p. 391.

138E.H. Gombrich, "*Icones Symbolicae*: The Visual Image in Platonic Thought," *Journal of the Warburg and Courtauld Institutes*, 11 (1948), 178.

139Bruno Snell, "Arcadia: The Discovery of a Spiritual Landscape," in *The Discovery of the Mind*, trans. by T.G. Rosenmeyer (New York, 1968), p. 306.

140Hallett Smith, "Elisabethan Pastoral," in *Pastoral and Romance*, ed. Eleanor Terry Lincoln, *ante cit.*, p. 17.

141Cf. *Ibid.*, p. 16.

142G.P. Lomazzo, *A Tracte Containing the Artes of Curious Paintings*, trans., Richard Haydocke (1598), sig. Bb6r.

143Shown in George Francis Hill (Keeper of Coins and Medals in the British Museum). *A Corpus of Italian Medals of the Renaissance Before Cellini* (London: British Museum, 1930), I, 67; II, 265.

144Harry B. Weille, *Great Paintings of the World* (New York: Harry N. Abrams, 1956), colorplate, no. 17.

145Christine Rees, "Some Seventeenth-Century Versions of the Judgment of Paris," *Notes and Queries*, "New Series," 24 (1977), 197.

146The reference is cited by Hallet Smith, *Elisabethan Poetry* (Cambridge, Mass., Harvard University Press, 1952), p. 5.

147Marsilio Ficino, *Opera* (Basle, 1576); *Epistolarum*. Lib. X, 919-920, cited by Christine Rees, *op. cit.*, p. 197.

148James M. Clark, *op. cit.*, p. 73.

149P.E. Cleator, *Weapons of War* (New York: Crowell, 1967), p. 107.

150*Hunter shooting an arbalest*, in Edwin Tunis, *Weapons, A Pictorial History* (Cleveland and New York: The World Publishing Co., 1954), p. 72.

151Picture held at the National Gallery of London and shown in Michael Levey, *Giotto to Cézanne*, p. 39, Plate 53.

152Salmen, *op. cit.*, Abbildung, 148, p. 203.

153Cf. Chandler R. Post, *Medieval Spanish Allegory* (Cambridge, Mass., 1915) and Gustavo Correa, "El concepto de la fama en el teatro de Cervantes," *Hispanic Review*, 27 (1959), 280-286; 299-302.

[154]Harold Bayley, *op. cit.*, p. 20.

[155]*Ibid.*, p. 21.

[156]Shakespeare, *The Merchant of Venice*, V. i. 90.

[157]Gustavo Correa, "El templo...," p. 64.

[158]Marsilio Ficino, *De vita coelitus comparanda* in *Opera Omnia* (Basle, 1576), p. 531 f., cited by E.H. Gombrich, *"Icones Symbolicae...,"* p. 176.

[159]*Ibid.*, p. 174.

[160]*Ibid.*

[161]Manuel Gómez Moreno, *The Golden Age of Spanish Sculpture* (Barcelona: Noguer, 1963; London: Thames and Hudson, 1964), pp. 44-45.

[162]James M. Clark, *op. cit.*, p. 67.

[163]*Ibid.*

[164]Fount at the end of the apse; see Philippe Ariès, *Western Attitudes Toward Death From the Middle Ages to the Present*, trans. Patricia M. Ramm, (Baltimore: Johns Hopkins University Press, 1974) pp. 32-33.

[165]T. Anthony Perry, *Erotic Spirituality: The Integrative Tradition from Leone Ebreo to John Donne* (University, Alabama: Alabama University Press, 1980), p. 5.

[166]See Daremberg et Staglio, *Dictionnaire des antiquités*, Paris, 1892; A. Pauly, *Real-Encyclopädie der classischen Alterthumswissenschaft*, Stuttgart, 1848, s.v. *Diana*; both works cited by Gustavo Correa, "El templo..." p. 64, n. 4.

[167]Harold Bayley, *op. cit.*, p. 24.

[168]Menéndez Pelayo, *Orígenes de la novela* (Santander: Consejo Superior de Investigaciones Científicas, 1943), II, pp. 248-49.

[169]Maxime Chevalier, "La *Diana* de Montemayor y su público en la España del siglo XVI," in *Creación y público en la literatura española*, ed. J.F. Botrel y S. Salaün (Madrid: Castalia, 1974), p. 45.

[170]Michel Zeraffa, "The Novel as Literary Form and as Social

Institution," in *Sociology of Literature and Drama*, ed. by Elisabeth and Tom Burns (Baltimore: Penguin, 1973), p. 35.

171Francisco López Estrada, "La epístola de Jorge Manrique a Diego Ramírez Pagán, " *Estudios dedicados a Ramón Menéndez Pidal*, 6 (1956), 406.

172Jean Subirats, "La *Diana* de Montemayor, roman à clef," in *Etudes Iberiques et Latino-américaines* (Paris: Publication de la Faculté des Lettres et Sciences Humaines de Poitiers, 1967), p. 114.

173Jean Subirats, *op. cit.*, p. 108. It should be pointed out that this is also frequently the plan of castles and palaces found in chivalric and sentimental literature of the Middle Ages and early Renaissance. See Howard R. Patch, "El otro mundo en la literatura medieval, seguido de un apéndice," in María Rosa Lida de Malkiel, *La visión de trasmundo en las literaturas hispánicas* (Mexico, 1956), pp. 203-204.

174Jean Subirats, *op. cit.*, p. 111.

175Michelle Débax, *Lexique de la "Diana" de Jorge de Montemayor* (Toulouse, 1971), I, p. xliii.

176Vicente Alvarez, *Relation du beau voyage que fit aux Pays Bas, en 1548, le prince Philippe d'Espagne, Notre Seigneur*, trad. M.T. Dovillée (Bruxelles, 1964), pp. 100, 105-106. To Maxime Chevalier goes the credit for relating the episode of the "salvajes" in *Diana* to the historical reference to the "wild men" in the feasts of Binche; see his *"La Diana* de Montemayor," *art. cit.*, p. 46.

177Daniel Heartz, "Un divertissement de Palais pour Charles Quint à Binche," in *Fêtes et cérémonies au temps de Charles Quint* (Paris, 1960), I, p. 338.

178*Ibid.*, II, Plate XXVII.

179*Ibid.*

180*Ibid.*, Plate XXVIII; cf. "Thournier, Kampff, und Ritterspiel. Episodes de l'Aventure du Château Ténébreux" (Binche, 1549). Shown in: Daniel Devoto, "Folklore et politique au Château Ténébreaux," in *Les fêtes de la Renaissance*, volume II: *Fêtes et cérémonies au temps de Charles Quint* (Paris:

Editions du Centre National de la Recherche Scientifique, 1960), Plates XXV and XXVI.

[181] John Block Friedman, *Orpheus in the Middle Ages* (Cambridge: Harvard University Press, 1970), p. 88.

[182] Cf. Michael Darbord, *La poésie religieuse espagnole des Rois Catholiques à Philippe II* (Paris: Institut d' Études Hispaniques, 1965), p. 421.

[183] John Block Freidman, *op. cit.*, pp. 38-85, especially, p. 79.

[184] *Ibid.*, p. 82.

[185] *Ibid.*, p. 76.

[186] Shown in W.K. C. Guthrie, *Orpheus and Greek Religion: A Study of the Orphic Movement.* (London: Methuen, 1935 / 1952), pp. 187-190; 371.

[187] Winternitz, *op. cit.*, Plate 30b.

[188] Michael Grant, "The Myth of Orpheus and Eurydice," *History Today*, June, 1967, pp. 372, 374, 379; see also W.K.C. Guthrie, *op. cit.*, Plate 3.

[189] "Egyptian hieroglyph showing a man playing a harp." Shown in: Sir E.A. Wallis Budge, *Egyptian Language: Easy Lessons in Egyptian Hieroglyphics* (New York: Dover Publications, Twelfth Impression, 1973 (originally published c. 1910), p. 45.

[190] See note 64, chapter I.

[191] Marqués de Santillana, *Obras* ed. Amador de los Ríos (Madrid, 1893), p. 423.

[192] Juan de Mena, *Laberinto de Fortuna*, ed. José Manuel Blecua (Madrid, 1943), p. 79.

[193] Fernando de Rojas, *La Celestina*, ed. Julio Cejador y Frauca (Madrid, 1962) II, p. 231.

[194] *Orphée et les muses. C'est la deduction du somptueux ordre...* Rouen, 1551. (Entrée d'Henri II, à Rouen, 1550). Shown in: Françoise Joukovsky, *Orphée et ses disciples dans la poésie française et néo-latine du XVIe siècle* (Genève: Librarie Droz, 1970), frontispiece.

[195] "Orphée dans un verger. *La tryumphante...entrée de... Monsieur Charles prince des hespaignes, Archiduc daustrice, en*

sa ville de Bruges, Paris, Gilles de Gourmont, 1515." Shown in: Françoise Joukovsky, *op. cit.*, p. 22.

196W.K.C. Guthrie, *Orpheus and the Greek Religion*, Plate 6.

197*Orpheus singing to Thracian Warriors*, shown in *World Music: An International Musical Anthology*, ed. by Ralph Brewster (Vienna, 1949), p. 13.

198Edward E. Lowinsky, "Music in Renaissance Culture," in *Renaissance Essays*, ed. Paul Oskar Kristeller and Philip R. Wiener (New York: Harper and Row, 1968), p. 350.

199Baldesar Castiglione, *The Book of the Courtier*, trans. Charles S. Singleton (New York: Doubleday, 1959) p. 75.

200Anríquez de Valderrábano, *Libro de música de vihuela intitulado "Silva de sirenas"* ("Valladolid, 1547), p. 29.

201Don M. Randel, "Sixteenth Century Spanish Polyphony and the Poetry of Garcilaso," *The Musical Quarterly*, 60 (1974), 77.

202Shown in Friedman, *Orpheus in the Middle Ages*, p. 154.

203Winternitz, *op. cit.*, p. 97; Plate 32 a.

204Guthrie, *op. cit.*, Plate 15.

205Friedman, *op. cit.*, p. 48.

206*Ibid.*, p. 77.

207*Ibid.*, p. 78.

208E.H. Gombrich, "*Icones Symbolicae*...," p. 169.

209Marcel Bataillon, *Erasmo y España: Estudios sobre la historia espiritual del siglo XVI*, trans. Antonio Alatorre (Mexico: Fondo de Cultura Económica 1966), p. 51.

210Jean Seznec, *op. cit.*, p. 100.

211*Ibid.*, p. 85.

212Pablo Cabañas, *op. cit.*, p. 15.

213*Ibid.*, p. 15.

214*Ibid.*, p. 16.

215*Ibid.*, pp. 153-157.

216Shown in Seznec, *op. cit.*, p. 113.

217*Medals*, p. 267.

218Gustavo Correa, "El templo...," p. 63.

219T. Anthony Perry *op. cit.*, p. 230.

220Cf. T.P. Harrison, Jr., "Shakespeare and Montemayor's

Diana," in *Texas University Studies in English*, 6 (1926), p. 98-99.

[221]An observation made already by David H. Darst, "Renaissance Platonism and the Spanish Pastoral Novel," *Hispania*, 52 (1969), 391.

[222]Walter R. Davis, *A Map of Arcadia: Sidney's Romance and Its Tradition* (New Haven: Yale University Press, 1965), p. 38.

[223]Cf. Erwin Panofsky, *Studies in Iconology. Humanistic Themes in the Art of the Renaissance* (New York: Oxford University Press, 1939), p. 55.

[224]See James Edward Congleton, *Theories of Pastoral Poetry in England, 1684-1798* (Gainesville, 1952), p. 26. This observation is also recorded by Evonne Patricia Buck in her fine doctoral dissertation (unpublished), "The Renaissance Pastoral Romance: A Study of Genre and Theme in Sannazzaro, Montemayor, Sidney and D' Urfé," (University of Michigan, 1975), p. 23.

[225]Philip Sidney, "Defense of Poetry," cited by James Edmund Congleton, *Theories of Pastoral Poetry, pp. 37-41;* see Evonne Patricia Buck, *op. cit.*, p. 23.

[226]Edward E. Lowinsky, *Secret Chromatic Art in the Netherlands Motet*, trans. Carl Buchman (New York: Russell-Russell, 1946), p. 135, n. 1.

[227]*Ibid.*, p. 153.

[228]Frederick A. de Armas, *op. cit.*, pp. 185-187.

[229]Américo Castro, *El pensamiento de Cervantes* (Barcelona, 1972), p. 145.

[230]Juan Bautista Avalle-Arce, *La novela pastoril española* (Madrid, 1959), 55-82.

[231]T. Anthony Perry, *op. cit.*, p. 233.

[232]Gustavo Correa, "El templo...," p. 74.

[233]On the "Water of Lethe," cf. Robert Graves, *The Greek Myths* (Baltimore: Penguin, 1955), I, p. 179.

[234]Erwin Panofsky, *Studies in Iconology*, p. 83.

235 Joseph R. Jones, "'Human Time' in *La Diana*" *Romance Notes*, 10 (1968), 145.
236 Erwin Panofsky, *Problems in Titian*, p. 131.
237 Jean Seznec *op. cit.*, p. 29.
238 *Ibid.*, p. 28.
239 Marion Lawrence, "Three Pagan Themes in Christian Art," in *De Artibus Opuscula XL...*, pp. 333-334.
240 *Ibid.*
241 Erwin Panofsky, *Studies in Iconology*, pp. 66ff.
242 Jean Seznec, *op. cit.*, p. 99.
243 W. Leonard Grant, *Literature and the Pastoral* (Chapel Hill, University of North Carolina Press, 1965), p. 9.
244 J. Hubert, *Les cryptes de Jouarre* (IVe Congrès de l'art du haut moyen-âge) (Melun: Imprimerie de la préfacture de Seine-et-Marne, 1952), cited in Philippe Ariès *op. cit.*, p. 29. The tomb of Venerable Agilbert, bishop of Dorchester and Paris, is found in the crypt of St. Paul's Church, Jouarre.
245 Philippe Ariès, *op. cit.*, p. 31.
246 In the text of this treatise reproduced by F.J. Sánchez Cantón, "Los trabajos de los Reyes, por Jorge de Montemayor," *Revista de Filología Española*, 12 (1925), p. 50. On the question of justice in *Diana*, Rachel Bromberg offers the following observation: "Felicia's palace is a composite of the House of Fortune, the Palace of Love, the House of Fame, the court, a Platonic academy, and a high den of witchery... All these layers of meaning have been gathered into one area for one purpose—to bring about a union between nature and fortune, of worth and luck; in short, to enact justice" (Rachel Bromberg, *Three Pastoral Novels* (Brooklyn, New York: 1969), p. 61.
247 John de Oliviera e Silva, "The *Arcadias* of Sir Philip Sidney in the context of the *Dianas* of Jorge de Montemayor and Gaspar Gil Polo: Religious Themes and the Language of Love" (Ph.D. diss., City University of New York, 1977), p. 14.
248 *Ibid.*, p. 56.
249 *Ibid.*
250 Bryant Lawrence Creel, *op. cit.*, p. 97.

[251] Rensselaer W. Lee, *op. cit.*, p. 211.
[252] T. Anthony Perry *op. cit.*, p. 232; see also 228.
[253] Walter R. Davis and Richard A. Lanham, *Sidney's Arcadia: A Map of Arcadia; Sidney's Romance in Its Tradition* (New Haven, 1965), p. 38.
[254] Joseph R. Jones, *op. cit.*, p. 146.
[255] T. Anthony Perry, *op. cit.*, p. 232.
[256] Rensselaer W. Lee, *op. cit.*, p. 211.

Notes to Conclusion

[1] Otis H. Green, "Courtly Love in the Spanish *Cancioneros*," *Publications of the Modern Languages Association*, 64 (1949), 258.
[2] Adolfo Salazar, *op. cit.*, p. 55.
[3] Nino Pirrotta, *op. cit.*, p. 22.
[4] This is exactly the situation in the *Quijote*, also, as Miguel Querol Gavaldá points out, *op. cit.*, p. 32.
[5] This is the title of the first essay in Romain Rollands's *Musiciens d'autrefois* (Paris, 1908), p. 27.

Ysopete-Zaragoza, 1489

hic liber confectus est
Madisoni .mcmlxxxiii.